John Newton: The Angry Sailor

John Newton: The Angry Sailor

by

Kay Marshall Strom

MOODY PRESS
CHICAGO

Library of Congress Cataloging in Publication Data

Strom, Kay Marshall, 1943-
John Newton, the angry sailor.

Summary: A biography of an eighteenth-century English clergyman whose early life was spent as an adventurous seafarer.
1. Newton, John, 1725-1807—Juvenile literature.
2. Church of England—England—Clergy—Biography—Juvenile literature. [1. Newton, John, 1725-1807.
2. Clergy] I. Title.
BX5199.N55S77 1984 283'.3 [B] [92] 83-23735
ISBN 0-8024-0335-2

7 9 10 8 6

Printed in the United States of America

Contents

1

Help!

"Father, I'm so scared!"

John huddled alone in a corner on the ship's deck. His small voice could barely be heard over the noise of the rolling thunder and the crashing sea.

Roaring waves pounded wildly against the sides of the wooden ship, rocking it back and forth so violently that at times the deck was completely under water. In the light made by a sudden flash of lightning, John could see the grim faces of the sailors who were struggling desperately to keep the ship afloat. But he didn't see his father anywhere. Could something have happened to him?

"Father!" John called out in terror. "Where are you, Father? Don't leave me now. Oh, please don't leave me!"

"I haven't left you, son," his father called back. "I'm over here working at the pump. If we don't keep the water out of this ship it will sink for sure."

"Oh, when will this awful storm end?" John cried.

"I don't know," answered his father. "I can

understand how terribly frightened you are, John. I'm frightened, too. We all are. But if you're going to be a sailor you must learn to work even when you're afraid. Now come over here and take your turn at the pump. The captain needs me down below."

Trembling with cold and fear, John stumbled over to the pump. There, hour after hour, he worked alone in the darkness. He shivered in his wet clothes, his arms ached terribly, and his hands were blistered and bleeding, but he dared not stop for even a moment's rest.

"Oh, how I wish I had stayed in school!" John cried miserably. "Even my schoolmaster's whip wasn't as bad as this horrible storm!"

The year was 1736, and John Newton was an eleven-year-old boy from London, England. Though he had never before been in a boat of any kind, John was trying hard to be a good sailor and to make his father proud of him.

Actually John was just now getting to know his father. Because Mr. Newton was a sailor by trade and was away at sea for months—sometimes even years—at a time, John had never had the chance to spend much time with him. Since John had no brothers or sisters, and since he had never been allowed to play with the neighbor children, John had spent almost all of his early years alone with his mother. But his mother loved him dearly, and he had been very happy.

Mrs. Newton never missed a chance to brag about her young son to anyone who would listen.

"John is so smart!" she would say proudly.

"He's going to be a great preacher some day, just you wait and see."

And it surely did seem that she was right. When he was only three years old, John was already reading quite well. By the age of four he had memorized whole chapters of Scripture, and at six he was learning Latin.

But then, thirteen days before John's seventh birthday, something happened that was to change his life completely. His mother died. To make matters worse, his father was at sea aboard a ship that was not due back in England for a year. There was no one who really wanted to take John in, but the little boy couldn't very well be left alone. So it was finally decided that several families would take turns keeping John. He stayed with a family until they grew tired of caring for him, and then he was sent off to live with someone else.

"I wish Father would come home!" John repeated again and again. "I know he would want me. If he was home I'd be happy again." And every night John would pray, "Dear Lord, please watch over my father. Take care of him and bring him safely back to me. And please, dear Lord, do it fast!"

In time Mr. Newton did get back to London, but things were not at all the way John had imagined they would be. For one thing, instead of just the two of them, there were three. Mr. Newton brought along a new lady friend.

"I don't like her!" John pouted to his father.

"I'm sorry to hear that," Mr. Newton replied, "because I'm going to marry her."

"But what about me?" John cried in alarm.

"What about you?" answered his father. "You'll stay here and get along with her whether you like her or not!"

But John soon found that getting along with her was not going to be easy. Soon after the wedding it became clear that the new Mrs. Newton cared nothing about her husband's sad, lonely young son. To her he was nothing but a nuisance. And it didn't take her long to convince her husband that John should be sent away to live at a boarding school where she wouldn't have to be bothered with him.

Now, the English boarding schools of those days were nothing like the schools children attend today. The schools 250 years ago were run by schoolmasters who could do anything they thought necessary to force the boys to learn. Most schoolmasters were very strict and quick to punish their students. Some were downright cruel, beating and whipping the boys regularly.

In John's class the boys were whipped whenever they made a mistake in their lessons. John wasn't used to that kind of treatment. The only teacher he had ever had was his mother, who was always gentle and kind. He was so afraid of his schoolmaster that whenever it was his turn to recite the lesson, he would forget everything he had learned. Of course that meant another whipping for him. No wonder John hated school.

After two years John refused to go back. "I hate it, Father!" he said. "If you send me back to that school I'll just run away. I can't stand another year with that mean old schoolmaster!"

"But if you don't go to school, what will you do?" asked Mr. Newton. "I'm going back to sea, so you can't stay here."

"Can I go to sea with you?" asked John. "I could learn to be a sailor, too."

"Well, now, that might not be a bad idea," answered Mr. Newton thoughtfully.

And that is how John Newton came to be on the ship.

When the worst of the storm had passed, John's father came back to the pump, where his son was still hard at work.

"You look tired, John," he said gently. "Go to your bunk and get a little sleep. I'll finish up here."

"Father," said John slowly, "I was sure that the ship would sink and we would all drown."

"This was your first experience with a storm at sea, John," answered his father. "The next one won't seem so bad. It won't take you long to learn all about being a sailor. And I know you will be a good one."

Mr. Newton was right. In the next few months John did learn a lot about the hardships of life at sea. There was much more to it than just keeping the ship afloat during a storm. Every day there were sails to mend, decks to scrub, fishing to do, food to cook, and dishes to wash. And John quickly learned that no matter how a sailor felt, he was always expected to do his share.

Then there were the days when the work was finished quickly. Those long days seemed to stretch out forever, for there was very little for a boy to do on board ship for weeks or months at a time. John spent many of those days sitting alone on the deck, staring out at the endless blue ocean, just thinking and remembering. He remembered his years as a happy, carefree little boy. He remembered his mother. How kind and gentle she had been! Could she look down from heaven and see him, he wondered? And if she could, was she disappointed that he wasn't in school learning to be a preacher? But then he remembered the boarding school and his cruel schoolmaster, and he was glad to be on board the ship.

Those days and those people were gone from John's life forever. London and everything he had ever known was far, far away. And what about God? Where was He? Was He far away too?

2

Kidnapped

Although the sun was just coming up on the distant horizon, the ship was already bustling with activity. John was supposed to be carrying buckets of water to the kitchen, but he paused long enough to watch the sun rise. To John it looked just like an enormous ball of fire coming straight up out of the sea.

"See that dark outline way out there, John?" asked his father, who had come up behind him. "That's Scotland. We'll be there tomorrow."

"Tomorrow?" asked John excitedly. "Will there be time to go ashore?"

"There sure will." His father laughed. "And will we have fun!"

"I can hardly wait!" John exclaimed.

This trip had been especially long and boring. It had been many months since John had seen anything but blue sea and blue sky, and he was ready for some excitement. In the port cities there was always plenty to see and do.

"I'm going to hurry up and finish my work so

that I can start getting ready!" John exclaimed as he ran off, water splashing after him.

"Not *too* fast," his father called after him with a laugh, "or you'll have to mop the deck, too."

When his work was done John hurried to his bunk, pulled the footlocker out from under it, and carefully took out his best clothes. Next he got a large basin from the kitchen. He filled it with hot water and gave himself a good scrubbing, taking special care to wash his neck and ears.

Many thoughts buzzed around in John's head as he tried to imagine all the exciting things that he and his father would see in the city. There would be sailors from every country in the world, and they would all have tales to tell. John loved to hear their exciting stories of pirates and whales and storms and treasures. Then there were the shops. He could get the new fishing knife he wanted. And the food! His mouth watered at the thought of all those delicious things to eat.

The next morning John was up long before daylight. "Get up, Father!" he whispered as he shook his father awake. "The sooner we get our work done, the sooner we can go ashore!"

It wasn't yet noon when John and his father left the ship. And what a perfect day it was! The weather was sunny and warm, and a gentle breeze was blowing. Not a cloud was in the sky. And the city! It was even better than John had imagined! He ran from one shop to another, not missing a single bakery or candy store.

"Don't spend all your money today, son." His

father laughed as John emerged with still another sugar roll.

"I can't help it, Father," John exclaimed. "Everything looks and smells so good! I'm tired of eating nothing but fish and biscuits."

Suddenly four huge sailors, dressed in the uniforms of the Royal Navy of the king of England, ran out from behind a tall building and grabbed John.

"This one looks good!" said the biggest sailor. He felt the muscles in John's arm and smiled. "What do you mates think?"

"Sure, he's just fine," the others agreed.

"You come with us!" ordered the first sailor, giving John a push.

"Where are you taking me?" asked John in a trembling voice.

"See that fighting ship in port?" asked a tall sailor with a long black beard. He pointed toward the harbor, down the very road that John and his father had just walked. "That's the *Harwich,* the biggest man-of-war in His Majesty's navy. It will be sailing early tomorrow morning, and when it does you'll be on board."

"Please don't take my son!" pleaded John's father. "He's only a boy!"

"If he's old enough to work, he's old enough for us," said the sailor. "We are under orders from the captain to find a new cabin boy, and I think that your son will do just fine."

"But I can't go with you on the man-of-war," said John, trembling even more. "I'm already working on a ship. My father is a sailor, too, and we work together."

"That may be what you *were* doing," replied the biggest sailor, "but from now on you'll be working on the king's warship. Don't you realize that French ships are right now anchored off the English coast? We could be at war any day!"

"But— but—" began John.

"It's your duty, boy!" interrupted the sailor. "And you have no choice. I hope you won't be foolish enough to argue or fight. If you do, you'll be punished as soon as we get on board. On a man-of-war, troublemakers are whipped at the whipping post!"

"Go quietly, John," whispered his father. He knew that the two of them could never hope to win against the four strong sailors. If they tried to fight, John might be killed. "You're a good sailor. If you cooperate, work hard, and always obey orders, the captain will make you an officer. I'm sure of it."

So young John Newton, frightened and confused, was marched aboard the man-of-war. With tears running down his cheeks, he turned for one last look at his father, who stood alone on the shore. There was just enough time to wave a sad good-bye.

"God be with you, son!" called his father. "God be with you!"

3

Aboard the Man-of-War

John's first day aboard the man-of-war was a total disaster. He worked hard, awfully hard, doing all the jobs no one else wanted to do. The sailors warned him that every job must be done perfectly or he would pay for it at the whipping post.

John tried to do well, he really did. But it was impossible to please everyone. Again and again poor John suffered the searing pain of the whip lashing across his bare back. It seemed the day would never end.

When all of the sailors had finished eating their evening meal, and when the dishes were finally washed and put away, the cook handed John a small plate of stew, a single biscuit, and a cup of cold coffee.

"Here's your supper, boy," he said. "Eat quickly. There's still a pile of pans for you to wash, and the kitchen floor must be scrubbed before you're finished for the night."

John was ravenously hungry. It only took a

minute for him to gulp down the stew, and the biscuit was polished off in one bite. Wiping his mouth on his sleeve he asked, "Can I have some more, sir? Please?"

"Hush, boy!" whispered the cook. "You don't ask for more."

"But, sir, I've been working hard all day. I need more food than this," insisted John.

Immediately two sailors jumped up and grabbed him. "If you were smart you'd be thanking the cook for what you got instead of demanding more!" said one.

"You obviously need a lesson in manners," added the other, "and we're just the ones to teach you."

With that John was given another whipping. But he did learn his lesson. That was the only time he asked for more food.

When the last pan was scrubbed clean and the floor was washed down, John was finally allowed to quit for the night.

"Here's where you'll sleep," said the cook, pointing to a spot on the floor. He threw John a blanket and left without so much as a good night.

Every muscle in John's exhausted body ached. But before lying down, John knelt to pray. "Please, dear God, please help me! Please take me away from this awful ship. Take me back to my father. If I stay here, I'll surely die!"

Even though John had always known about God, it had been a long time since he had done any praying. It was not that he had forgotten all the things that his mother had so carefully taught him;

it was just that God seemed so far away and unimportant in his life. That's obviously the way his father felt, too. Although Mr. Newton was a good man, he never mentioned God at all, nor had John ever seen him read his Bible or heard him pray. But now that his father was far away and John had no one to help him, his thoughts went back to something his mother had taught him—that nothing could ever separate him from God's love and care.

Surely God will hear my prayers, John thought. *Surely He will get me off this terrible warship.*

Never once did John stop to think that God might have other plans for him.

That night as he slept, John dreamed about his mother and about the peaceful and happy life he had when she was alive. But his dreams ended abruptly when a large, rough sailor awakened him with a hard kick.

"Get up, you lazy boy!" he growled. "It's almost five o'clock in the morning! Why aren't you up and working?"

For a minute John couldn't remember where he was. Sitting up, he rubbed his sleepy eyes and stared blankly at the unfriendly face glaring down at him.

"Come on! Get moving!" ordered the sailor. He pulled John to his feet and pushed him toward the kitchen. "You're supposed to be helping get breakfast ready. Hurry up! We're hungry!"

John stumbled toward the kitchen. A large pot of wheat cereal was already boiling on the stove.

At least now I'll get something to eat, John thought as he stared longingly at the bubbling pot.

But as if he could read John's thoughts, the

cook's helper menacingly waved a large knife in John's face and growled, "I'm in charge of the food in here! If you dare to take so much as one taste of anything, I promise you that you'll never do it again!" And he really looked as though he meant it.

John swallowed hard and tried to answer. "Yes, sir," he gulped, but his voice was hardly more than a whisper.

All day long John worked in the steaming heat of the kitchen. He carried huge, heavy pots of boiling food back and forth from the wood-burning stove. He washed the dishes, scoured the pans, and mopped the floor. He scrubbed vegetables and kept the stove filled with wood. There were animals on the ship that would be used for meat during the long voyage, and John was put in charge of them. "If any of them die," he was warned, "it'll come out of your hide."

The sailors were given two meals a day, breakfast and supper. They worked hard, and they ate a lot. John was not allowed to eat until everyone else was finished. If there was nothing left, he was told, he would have to be satisfied with whatever scraps he could find on the men's plates.

"Why can't we just divide the food up equally?" John asked. "Then I could get my share like everyone else."

"Because you're not important to this ship," answered the cook. "The captain can always get another cabin boy in any port city. That's how he got you, remember. But it's a lot harder to replace the experienced sailors. So if anyone has to go hungry, you can be sure it won't be them."

It was late at night when John was finally allowed to stop work and go to his sleeping place on the floor. This time he didn't take time to pray. He was much too tired to even dream.

Days, weeks, and months went by with little change. John was always awakened long before dawn and made to work hard until late at night. It seemed that he had barely fallen asleep when he was again awakened with a kick.

"My life couldn't be more miserable," John complained to a young sailor who had befriended him.

"Of course it could," his friend sneered. "Don't be such a baby."

John's new friend was a wild young man. None of the other sailors liked him at all.

"Look at me," he continued. "I get more beatings and whippings than any other man on this ship. I'm much more miserable than you are!"

"Why are you always doing things that you know will get you into trouble?" John asked.

"I do exactly what I want to do," the young sailor snapped. "I'm not about to let anyone boss me around."

"But it's important for a sailor to obey orders," John said, "That's the very first rule my father taught me."

"Why should I take orders from anyone?" sneered his friend. "There's only one person who cares about me, and that's me. If I don't watch out for myself, it's sure that no one else will. And don't you start warning me about God. I'm not stupid enough to believe in Him!"

The more friendly John got with the young sailor, the more like him he became. He began to copy his rudeness, his disobedience, and his rough language. He also began to copy his dislike for God.

In December the *Harwich* was in port for one day. Since they wouldn't be in port again for a long, long time, John and his friend persuaded the captain to let them go ashore. "Just be sure you're back by sunset and not one minute later!" he warned them.

But once on shore the two young sailors went wild. They stole from the shops and the market booths. They untied horses, then they laughed out loud as their owners helplessly chased them down the street. Their idea of fun was to do anything they could dream up to cause trouble.

The day passed quickly—too quickly. When the sun began to set, they still were in no mood to return to the ship. But John reluctantly suggested, "We'd better be getting back."

"Not yet!" his friend argued. When he saw John's doubtful look he laughed. "Don't worry. The captain will wait."

It was early morning and the sun was just rising in the eastern sky when John and his friend finally stumbled back aboard the ship.

"Where have you two been?" the captain roared, his eyes flashing with anger.

"On shore." John's friend laughed. "What of it?"

At that the captain shook with rage. "Take them to the whipping post!" he ordered.

John howled with pain as the whip lashed again and again across his bare back. But though their punishment was terrible, it could have been much worse. The captain could have ordered them killed for desertion. Because he was a kind man, and because he had been very much impressed with John's ability as a sailor, he hadn't done so. But his feelings toward John were changed completely, for John had proved himself to be an undependable troublemaker.

"If there was a God in heaven who loved me, He wouldn't let me suffer so much," John said bitterly. "He would have taken me away from this horrible ship. That's what I asked Him to do in the first place."

Right then and there John made a decision that was to change his life forever. "Since God can't—or won't—take care of me, then I'll just have to take care of myself. From now on I'll be as mean and as tough as any sailor alive!"

4

Escape

"All hands on deck!" ordered the first mate. "Man your stations! A storm is blowing up from the north!"

John joined the other men in a scramble up the narrow stairway and onto the deck.

"Over here!" called John's friend. He and several other sailors were battling the billowing sails in an effort to get them down before the winds ripped them to pieces. "This storm blew up so fast that these sails are already badly damaged."

"Looks like we'll be mending sails tomorrow," said John.

"We'll be lucky if ripped sails is the worst thing that happens," said an old, white-haired sailor. "This storm looks to be a real bad one."

John glanced out at the crashing waves, then up at the dark sky. It was hard to believe that it was only noon—it looked more like midnight. In an effort to protect himself from the rain, which was now pouring down in torrents, he turned up his collar and pulled his hat down over his eyes. Then he set to work. By now John had been through so many storms that even the rough ones didn't much worry him anymore.

A huge wave crashed against the side of the ship, knocking it violently to one side.

"Be careful!" the old sailor called. "I've seen many a man washed overboard in conditions like this. You'd do well to tie yourselves to the railing."

"I can't work when I'm tied to the railing," John's friend complained. "It's too uncomfortable."

"Uncomfortable or not, you'd better do it," the old sailor warned. "I've been through many more storms than you have, son, and believe me, I know what I'm talking about."

"You worry too much, old man!" the young sailor snapped. "Leave me alone! I can take care of myself."

Those were the last words he ever said. At that very instant another wave—a truly enormous one—swept over the deck, washing John's friend right off and into the raging sea.

"We must save him!" John cried as he rushed to the railing. "Somebody do something!"

"There's nothing we can do," said the old sailor shortly. "He was a fool, always insisting on doing everything his own way. He never would listen to anyone. Well, he did it his own way, all right, and you can see what happened."

"And good riddance, if you ask me!" stated another sailor. "We'll all be better off without that troublemaker."

The storm passed quickly, but it was a long, long

time before John could get his friend's death out of his mind. Day after day he stood at the railing, staring silently out to sea. And night after night he relived the horror in his nightmares. Could it be that God was trying to warn him about the dangers of his own behavior? If so, John wasn't listening.

Every day aboard the man-of-war became more unbearable for John. Finally he decided that he could stand it no longer. The ship was due in port the next day, and very carefully John began to make plans to escape.

John got up very early the next morning. Finishing his chores quickly, he prepared to go ashore just as he always did. When he left the ship, it was with a group of other sailors. He was very careful not to do anything that would cause suspicion.

Once away from the ship John wandered around town, visiting the various shops. Though he looked like just another sailor enjoying a day in port, all the time he was waiting and watching for a chance to get away from the other men.

When a traveling musician came down the street singing and dancing, everyone crowded around to listen. This was just the chance John had been waiting for. He turned and walked quickly down the street in the opposite direction. When he thought he was far enough away to avoid attracting attention, he broke into a run.

John ran as fast and as far as he could. Finally he could run no more. Dropping down by the side of the road, he closed his eyes, gasping for breath. His head throbbed and his lungs ached. He could hardly breathe, and his legs wouldn't move. For a long time he lay perfectly still.

After he had rested for a while John sat up and, for the first time, looked around him. The crowded city had been left far behind. He was all alone on a little country road. In every direction there was nothing to be seen but rolling hills and swaying wheat fields. Just up ahead John noticed an old abandoned barn—a perfect place to spend the night.

"I made it!" John exclaimed out loud. "I really made it. I've actually managed to escape from that awful ship. It'll be out to sea before anyone realizes that I'm gone. Even if they do miss me, they surely won't take the time to search this far. I'm free at last!"

Once inside the barn John made himself a comfortable bed of thick straw. Sighing deeply, he settled down and drifted off into a sound and peaceful sleep.

Hours later John awakened with a start. Had he heard something, or was he just dreaming? No, there it was again. It was voices, and they sounded like they were just outside the barn. Who could it be? John lay perfectly still, hardly daring to even breathe.

"Let's look in this old barn," someone called.

John gasped in horror. He knew that voice! It was one of the sailors from the man-of-war. There was no time to think. John jumped to his feet and leaped through a back window.

"There he goes!" yelled the sailor.

"Grab him!" shouted another one. "Don't let him get away!"

To his horror, John saw that he was completely surrounded. Sailors were coming at him from all sides. Confused and frightened, he made one last desperate attempt at escape. Leaping the fence, he ran out of the barnyard and across the road.

If I can just make it to one of those fields, he thought, *I might be able to hide among the tall wheat stalks.*

Unfortunately the men guessed John's plan, and they headed him off. There was no way out. Terror gripped John as the angry men jumped on him. They threw him to the ground and held him tight.

"You were a fool to try to escape!" snarled one sailor.

"Don't you know how much the king hates deserters?" shouted another. "You can count yourself lucky if you're still alive tomorrow morning."

5

The Angry Sailor

"Now let's see you try to escape!" taunted the sailors. John's arms and legs had been bound with chains so heavy that he could hardly move. Dragging him to his feet, his captors marched him back to town and down the main street as if he were the worst of criminals. All along the way people stopped and stared at him. John hung his head in shame and fear, but inside he was burning up with anger and hatred.

Instead of being returned to the ship, John was taken to the guardhouse in town. The sailors shoved him inside with about ten other prisoners, then the door was slammed shut and tightly bolted.

For a long time the other prisoners just stared at him in silence. Finally a tough-looking character with a long scar over one eye stepped up and demanded, "What're you in here for?"

"I deserted my ship," John replied.

"And what ship might that be?" the man asked.

"It's the *Harwich,*" John answered. "His Majesty's ship the *Harwich.*"

"The *Harwich?*" the man exclaimed in surprise. "Isn't that a warship?"

"Yes," said John.

At that the man broke out into wild laughter. He laughed and he laughed, and before long everyone else was laughing too. Everyone, that is, except John. He had no idea what the big joke was.

"You mean to say you deserted a warship?" the scarred prisoner demanded. "You must be as dumb as they come! Don't you know what happens to deserters? They are put to death!"

"Maybe they're going to leave me here instead of taking me back to my ship," John said hopefully. "If I'm not taken back to my ship I won't be killed, will I?"

The man didn't answer. Apparently he was tired of talking. He sat down, pulled a long knife from his left boot, and started cutting his grimy fingernails. No one else seemed interested in talking, either, so John was left to consider his fate alone.

For the rest of the day John restlessly paced the floor of the guardhouse. Then, just before dusk, the ship's guards returned. John's heart sank at the sight of them. So he wasn't going to be left behind after all. Still bound in chains and irons, John was marched back toward the ship.

"Good-by, deserter!" called the scarred prisoner. "Good-by and good luck. You'll need it!" At that he again broke out laughing. And again the other prisoners joined in. Their mocking laughter followed John out of the guardhouse and all the way up the street.

When they got back to the ship, John was startled to see that all of the other sailors were standing along the ship's deck. They were actually waiting for him to be brought aboard. There they stood, staring at him sullenly. Some kicked him as he went by. Others threw rocks or shouted insults. It hardly seemed possible that these men were the same ones with whom John had lived and worked for so many months.

John was taken straight to the whipping post and, without a word, tied up securely. There he was whipped over and over and over again. Although he had felt the searing pain of that whip many times before, it had never been as bad as this.

"Please have mercy on me!" John cried. But his cries only seemed to make the men angrier.

"There is no mercy for a deserter!" they yelled back at him.

"I was going to make you an officer on this ship," shouted the captain. "But now—if you are lucky enough to survive—you'll spend the rest of your life in misery. The worst jobs we can find will be given to you to do. You have proved that you are nothing but a coward and an idiot, and from now on that is exactly how you will be treated."

That night John Newton lay alone on the cold deck of the ship. He had been whipped so badly that the sailors, thinking that surely he must be dead, had finally left him alone.

Through the entire ordeal, not one man had done a single thing to help John. It was true that because of his behavior and his attitude John didn't have very many friends among the sailors. But he did have a few. And there were some men who were always ready to offer a helping hand to anyone who was in trouble no matter what he had done. But the captain had been so angry with John that he had given strict orders forbidding anyone to do a thing to ease John's suffering. They were not even allowed to speak to him or to give him a drink of water.

For a long time John lay on the deck, unable to move. He was still laying there when the sailors raised anchor and the ship slowly sailed out of the harbor. John managed to lift his head just in time to see the shore disappearing into the distance. With it went all hope of escape.

What a failure I am! John thought bitterly. *Not only have I failed to get off this ship, but because I tried to escape, my life as a sailor will be much worse than it ever was before.*

In great pain, John pulled himself up and looked toward the sky. His eyes flashed with anger, and his mouth twisted in hatred.

"There is no God in heaven!" he gasped. "And even if there was, I would hate Him for letting this happen to me!"

Then, falling back to the deck, he buried his head in his hands and wept bitterly.

Many hours passed before John was finally able to drag himself to his feet. Through a great deal of effort he struggled to the ship's railing. Not a single person was in sight.

"My life is miserable, and it sure won't be getting any better," John moaned. "The captain hates me. He will never, ever make me an officer. And I don't have any hope of escaping now, for they'll be watching me constantly. There is only one way out for me. I'll jump overboard and drown myself in the sea. That's the only way I can ever hope to put an end to my sorrows and sufferings."

That's what John Newton decided, and that's what he fully intended to do. But for some reason, he didn't. Why not? Again and again John asked himself that question, but it was to be many years before he knew the answer.

From that day on John faced constant ridicule and scorn from his shipmates. Every day he was forced to work harder, and every day the officers found worse jobs for him to do. The captain was determined to make an example of John Newton. Deserters would not be tolerated on his ship.

As for John, he became more and more angry and more and more hateful. He was always fighting with the other sailors. He stole from everyone. He lied and he cheated. One of his favorite pastimes was to make up lies that would cause innocent sailors to be punished at the whipping post. Of course he always watched such punishments from the front row. If the sailor cried out in pain, John would laugh out loud.

It wasn't only the other sailors who fell under John's terrible anger, either. Very often he would shake his fist toward heaven and shout out his hatred to God.

6

Mary Catlett

When the ship docked in London, John begged to be allowed to go ashore to visit with his father and his friends. The captain finally agreed to let him go but only on the condition that a guard would be with him every minute.

"If he tries to escape," the guard was ordered, "shoot him!"

John's old friends in London couldn't believe that this wild seventeen-year-old, so full of hatred and anger, was the same John Newton they had known all their lives.

"He's gone crazy!" they whispered to each other. "He's turned into a wild madman."

John hadn't seen his father since that terrible morning when he was forced to join the crew of the *Harwich,* and he could hardly wait to see him again.

"But how will I explain you to my father?" John asked his guard. "It would hurt him terribly to know how much trouble I've gotten myself into."

"You don't have to tell him who I am," the guard replied kindly. "Just say that I'm a friend of yours."

As it turned out, the visit with his father was very disappointing. John's stepmother never left them alone for a single minute. She hadn't liked him very much when he was a little boy, and now that he was a wild teenager she liked him even less. Of course John wasn't fond of her, either. He was convinced that she had taken all his father's love and attention, leaving none for him. And she was the one who had insisted that he be sent away to boarding school. He would never forgive her for that. Cutting his visit short, John said good-by and prepared to leave.

"John, do you remember Mr. and Mrs. Catlett who live in Kent?" Mr. Newton suddenly asked. "They want you to come to their home for a visit before you leave London."

"I don't remember them," John replied.

"They were your mother's best friends," Mr. Newton continued.

"I don't know—" said John slowly. Why would he want to spend his time visiting some old friends of his mother? Surely he could find something more exciting than that to do in London.

"They really would like to see you," John's father insisted. "You wouldn't have to stay long. It would mean a lot to them." Then with a smile he added, "I know they would want to fix you a delicious dinner."

"I'll think about it," said John.

Actually Jonn had no intention whatsoever of wasting his shore leave at the Catletts' house, but for some reason that's exactly what he ended up doing. Maybe, because he was so determined to keep

John out of trouble, the guard talked him into going. Maybe it was the thought of a good, home-cooked meal that persuaded him to go. Or maybe it was the hand of God.

When John arrived at the Catlett home he was welcomed like a long lost child. They were so happy to see him! Besides Mr. and Mrs. Catlett, there were two girls in the family. Mary, the oldest, was fourteen, and from the moment John first set eyes on her he knew that he was in love. Of course he was very careful not to let anyone know how he felt.

"You want to know something funny, John?" asked Mrs. Catlett. "When you were a very little boy and Mary was just a baby, your mother and I had great ideas for the two of you. We had it all planned that you would grow up friends and then someday that you would be married."

Everyone laughed. John tried to laugh, too, but he could feel his face growing hot. How he hoped it didn't show!

"Hush, dear," Mr. Catlett said to his wife. "You are embarrassing the boy."

"Nonsense," she replied. "They were only babies." Then turning to John she added, "Your mother had it all worked out. You two would live right here in Kent or in London. She had her heart set on your being a preacher, you know, John."

"A preacher!" exclaimed John's guard. "John Newton a preacher?" He burst out laughing at the very idea. But John shot a look at him that was so threatening that he stopped short. After that he didn't even dare smile.

All the time that he was with Mary, John was like

a different person. He became as quiet and as gentle and as kind as Mary herself. The guard was so surprised and impressed by the change in John that he decided that perhaps John might be more dependable than he had thought. He even allowed John and Mary some time alone.

"Do you ever think about being a preacher like your mother wanted you to be?" Mary asked.

"Me? A preacher?" John asked bitterly. "Listen, after all I've been through I just hope that there is no God!"

"Why?" asked Mary.

"Because if there is a God, then He either cares nothing at all about me or else He has no power to help me. Either way, I wouldn't want to know Him."

When John's ship was again ready to sail, Mary went along to the London dock to say good-by.

"I'm so glad I met you, John," she said. "I only wish you weren't so angry toward God. He is the only one who can help you with your problems, you know."

"Help me!" said John angrily. "If there is a God at all, then He is the one who allowed all my problems to start in the first place."

"You only think that because you don't understand the way God is working in your life," said Mary softly. Then she added, "I'm going to make you a promise, John. I promise that I will pray for you every single day that you're gone. I'm going to pray that He will keep you safe, and I'm going to pray that He will prove to you that He truly does love you and that you do need Him."

Back at sea John thought about Mary constantly, but he mentioned his feelings to no one. He was certain that he would gladly give anything—even his very life—for her. But unfortunately John's love didn't change the way he lived. Away from Mary, John was worse than ever.

7

Get Rid of Him

"A sailor must always obey, John," said the captain. "There are no exceptions to this rule—especially on a battleship."

When John was first told to report immediately to the captain's office he was sure that he was in big trouble. But now as he stood before him, John was amazed to find that the captain didn't seem at all angry. His voice was quiet and controlled. He did seem unusually serious, though, and instead of looking John straight in the eye, he kept staring down at his folded hands.

"You know this rule perfectly well," the captain continued, "and you know the reasons for it. Yet you steadfastly refuse to obey. I have threatened you, I have punished you, and I have had you whipped repeatedly. Still your behavior gets worse and worse every single day. I've finally come to the conclusion that as a sailor you are completely hopeless."

John listened in silence, his head bowed. If the captain truly had given up on him, he dreaded the thought of what would happen next. It was possible that the captain might even have him put to death. After all, John had deserted the ship at a time when there were threats of war.

"We're having problems with the ship's steering, so we have to go back to London for repairs," the captain continued. "As soon as we are in port I want you off this ship, and I don't ever want to see you again."

For a moment John just stared in surprise. Then he laughed out loud. "Is that all? You're only going to put me off the ship?" He sneered. "Well, for your information that suits me just fine! I've tried for years to get away from here!"

"It looks like you've finally succeeded," replied the captain with a sigh. Then, after a pause, he looked at John and asked, "What are you going to do now?"

"I'll get onto another ship, of course," answered John rudely. "Only this time it will be one where I can be an officer. Then I'll be giving the orders and everyone will have to obey me."

The captain shook his head slowly. "Unless you mend your ways, John," he said, "you're headed for a life full of sorrow and trouble."

"What do you know about life?" he snapped. "You're nothing but a worn-out old man!" Then he turned on his heel and, without so much as a salute or a good-by, he was gone.

Once on shore, John began to have second thoughts about his life as a sailor. Did he really want to always be away at sea like his father was? He did, after all, have Mary Catlett to consider. She was all he had been able to think about lately. Maybe he should just marry her and settle down in London.

The more John thought about marriage, the more he liked the idea. And so, with that in mind, he hurried off to see his father and to tell him about his decision.

"Mary Catlett is the most wonderful girl in the world, Father, and I'm going to marry her," John announced.

"But, John," Mr. Newton answered in surprise, "do you realize how young she is? She's only fourteen years old! And you're only seventeen. If you go over to her house and make such a suggestion to her father, he'll throw you out for sure."

"What do you know about it?" John shouted angrily. "I'm going over there right now to tell Mr. and Mrs. Catlett that I'm going to marry their daughter. And you can't change my mind." With that John stomped out of his father's house.

Of course Mr. Newton was right. When John told Mary's parents what he had in mind, her father was furious.

"I want you out of my house!" Mr. Catlett ordered. "And don't bother to come back again!"

Mary's mother, however, was much more understanding. "Are you sure that you have really thought this through, John?" she asked gently. "You and Mary have only known each other for a very short time, you know. And of course my husband is right—Mary is much too young for marriage. You both are."

John hung his head in embarrassment. "I'm

sorry I asked," he said quietly.

"Perhaps things will be different when you're both older," Mrs. Catlett suggested. "If you still feel the same way in a couple of years, and if Mary agrees, we can talk about it again."

"But until then," Mr. Catlett added quickly, "I think that it would be best if you didn't come to visit anymore."

"Mary knows how you feel about her," explained Mrs. Catlett. "Please don't make it hard on her by mentioning anything about marriage just yet."

"I think you should leave now before she gets home," Mr. Catlett said firmly.

John left, but he certainly didn't feel like going back to face his father and having to admit that he was wrong. There was only one other place to go—to the docks. A ship was leaving that very day for Venice, Italy, and it had room on board for one more deck hand.

"I've always wanted to see Italy," John said. And so, without a word to Mary or his father, John signed aboard.

When the ship sailed, John stood alone on the deck watching London fade into the distance. He knew that it would be a long, long time before he would see Mary again. Maybe he never would. That thought caused him indescribable loneliness and pain.

"Get to work, sailor!" ordered the captain's assistant, who had come up behind John. "We didn't take you aboard to have you stand around staring back at London!" With that he gave John a shove toward the forward deck where the other men were already hard at work.

John whirled around and glared furiously at the officer. "No one pushes me around!" he shouted, holding his ground. He raised his fists, preparing for a fight.

"You know who you've got there, don't you?" asked a short, fat sailor who happened to walk by just at that moment. "That's the troublemaker who was thrown off the *Harwich!*"

"Oh, he is, is he?" said the officer. Turning to John he growled, "Don't you try making trouble here. We won't put up with it!"

The crew on this ship was a tough bunch of sailors, and it wasn't long before John had made enemies of every single one of them. They despised John, and John hated them. But of the entire crew, the person John hated the most was the captain himself, for John held him entirely responsible for his increasing unhappiness.

As his hatred grew, John carefully devised a wicked plan to organize a mutiny, kill the captain, and take over the ship. He was not the least bit afraid of God, and he certainly wasn't afraid of any man. He was not even particularly concerned about what might happen to him. But there was one thing that did cause him worry.

Even if I am able to kill the captain, it's still very possible that I couldn't get the other men to join me in taking over the ship, John reasoned. *And if they wouldn't join me, then they would probably kill me for revenge. In time Mary would certainly hear all the details about my death—they would call it treason. I just can't stand the idea of Mary being sad and hurt and disappointed in me after I'm dead!*

It was that thought alone that kept John from carrying out his murderous plan.

Every day John became meaner and more troublesome. Finally he got so bad that even those tough sailors could stand him no longer.

"Hail the next ship that passes," ordered the captain, "and offer to trade John Newton for any man they want to get rid of."

Now it just happened that the next ship to pass had a man on board who was desperately ill and needed to be returned to England immediately. Although no ship's crew wanted to be bothered with having to care for a man that sick, the captain was so anxious to have John off his ship that he would have agreed to anything. And so the exchange was made.

"At last we are rid of you!" shouted the sailors to John as the two ships began to sail apart.

"And I am rid of you!" John yelled back. "Now I can do anything I want! No one will ever give me orders again!"

8

Island of the Slaves

In John Newton's day there were many, many ships sailing the seas. Before there were airplanes and railroads, sailing was the only method of transportation between many countries. Of course there were navy vessels like the one John was on—most countries had battleships of some kind—but there were also merchant ships, cargo ships, passenger ships, and even the dreaded pirate ships. But the most hated of all were the slave ships, and it was to a slave ship that John had been traded.

It was the captain himself who first greeted John aboard. "What's your name, boy?" he asked.

"John Newton, sir," came the reply.

The captain raised his eyebrows in surprise. "Did you say John Newton? Why, I do believe that I know your father! In fact, he and I are old friends. Welcome to our ship, John. If you're half the sailor your father is, we're lucky to have you aboard."

"Where are we headed?" John asked.

"For the coast of Africa, of course," the captain replied with a smile. "This is a slave ship, remember? We're on our way to collect a load of slaves." Then he asked, "Have you ever been to Africa?"

"No," John answered, "but I'm ready to go."

With a jolly laugh the captain clamped his huge arm around John's shoulders and gave him a tight hug. "That's what I like to hear!" he exclaimed. "I can see that we're going to get along just fine. You come and eat with me in my cabin tonight. There will be plenty of time for work tomorrow."

Could this be true? Even though the captain had been fully informed of John's troublesome behavior, he was actually willing to overlook all of those past mistakes and to accept him as a friend. This was John's big chance. If he was ever going to prove himself worthy to serve as an officer, this was surely the time.

But unfortunately John had learned nothing from his past. As soon as the captain turned to go, John sneered under his breath, "What an old fool you are! Why would I ever want you for a friend? I intend to do exactly as I please, and you had better not try to order me around." Then, after glancing around the ship, he added with a sharp laugh, "Why, they don't even have a whipping post here. This is the place for me, all right."

Not only was John meaner and more troublesome than ever, but he immediately began to provoke and encourage all the other sailors to act in the same way. He refused to obey orders, and he dared anyone to try to force him to do anything he didn't want to do. He was always ready to fight anyone, and because he had so much practice, it was seldom John Newton who got hurt.

The captain was baffled at John's behavior. He was alarmed to see that the other sailors were already following his terrible example of laziness, dishonesty, and disobedience. But despite his enormous size and his rough appearance, the captain was a gentle, peaceable man. He had no idea how to control this wild young sailor, so he did nothing, hoping that John would soon come to his senses. John, however, took this as a sign of weakness and began to mock the captain openly.

Needless to say the captain no longer looked upon John as a friend. One day, in utter frustration, he shouted out in anger, "I wish I had never set eyes on you, John Newton! You're a curse to any ship you board. This is a fine way to thank me for offering you my friendship."

"So I'm a curse, am I?" John laughed rudely. "And you think that I should be thankful to you? Well, now, maybe you're right. I do like the sound of your words. In fact, I like them so much that I think I'll make them into a song. I'll call it, '*John, the Thankful Curse.*' "

Right then and there John sat down on a crate, took out a pen and paper, and wrote out his song. He was careful to see that it ridiculed the captain in the most embarrassing and humiliating ways possible. Then, when the song was done, John called the other sailors together and taught it to them. After that, whenever the captain walked by, the sailors would join together and sing John's song as loudly as they could. They didn't want the captain to miss one single word.

Finally, after many months, the slave ship

dropped anchor at an island off the coast of Africa. As John stepped ashore he noticed that another slave ship was in the process of being loaded with its cargo of captive black men, women, and children who had been kidnapped from their homes and sold to slave traders. The slave traders then sold them to the slave ships. John stopped to watch.

"Chain them together," the captain ordered. "I don't want any trouble from them. Come on! You can get more than that in there! Pack them in!"

John was amazed at how many people were being pushed and shoved down into the hold of the ship. "They'll never survive the trip," he exclaimed to a sailor who was standing next to him.

"Enough of them will." The sailor laughed. "Even if only half of them make it, we'll still earn a handsome profit."

When it was impossible to squeeze in one more person, the door was slammed shut and securely bolted. There the captives would remain until the ship arrived at its destination, usually England or America. The trip would take many months. When the weather was hot, it would be like an airless oven down in the ship's hold. When the weather was cold, the captives would come close to freezing.

"Where are you headed?" John asked.

"To America," the sailor answered. "New Orleans."

"It doesn't seem like they'll be in any condition to sell by the time you get there," John said.

"Maybe not when we get there," the sailor replied, "but after we unload the survivors we'll work on them for a month or so, getting them fattened up and healthy. You'd be surprised at the price they'll fetch in the slave market."

"Who will you sell them to?" John asked.

With a laugh the sailor answered, "To anyone who can afford their price."

Three days before John's ship was ready to sail, the captain died. For John, this was a very bad turn of events. Though the captain disliked him greatly, he put up with him because of his friendship with John's father. But the first mate—the one who would now be taking over as the new captain—made his position perfectly clear.

"Unless you change your ways, John Newton," he said firmly, "I'll have you thrown overboard and left to drown in the sea. And don't you think for a minute that I won't do it, because I will."

There were many white men who had settled in different places along the African coast and also on the islands around it. Most of those white men worked in the slave business. Some were slave traders who bought the Africans from the kidnappers, locked them up, and prepared them for sale to the slave ships. Since the slaves were sold for a great deal more money than was paid for them, most of the slave traders were very wealthy men.

The day after the captain's death, John met the slave trader who lived with his African wife on this particular island.

"Why do you want to work so hard on that ship?" the slave trader asked John. "Only a fool would work like that for so little money."

"I don't like it," said John, "but there's nothing I can do about it."

"You could stay on this island with us," replied the slave trader. "There's hardly any work to do around here, and the slave business would make you a rich man."

"Well," said John thoughtfully. "I'll have to admit that I'm not very happy about spending months and months with that new captain ordering me around."

"On our island you wouldn't have anyone giving you orders," said the slave trader. "In fact, you would be the one doing the ordering! Except for my wife and myself, everyone here is a slave. They do what they're told to or they die!"

"It surely does sound like a good life," John admitted. "There are two things that I really hate. I hate being poor, and I hate being told what to do. I've always wanted to be rich and to do whatever I please."

"So you've made up your mind then?" asked the trader. "You'll stay?"

"Yes," answered John. "I'll stay."

"Good!" replied the trader. He grabbed John's hand and shook it hard. While they were still shaking hands, the slave trader suddenly broke into a loud laugh. He laughed harder and harder and harder. Then his wife joined in. Soon John was laughing, too, although he wasn't quite sure what it was that was so terribly funny.

9

Prisoner!

Although the slave ship wasn't scheduled to leave for another two days, John lost no time in collecting his belongings and moving out. He couldn't wait to explore his new island home.

"The next time any of you see me, I'll be a rich man," John bragged to the other sailors. "That's because I'm not a fool like all the rest of you. Only fools let other men boss them around. On this island I'm going to be the one giving the orders. So if you ever want to come back, you had better be ready to take orders from me!"

Even though this was the largest of the Plantane Islands, it took John just a little over an hour to walk the entire way around it. The ground was very sandy, and palm trees grew everywhere. After exploring the island, John chose a site to build a house for himself. The spot he chose was not too far from the home of the slave trader and his wife, but it was not too close, either. He had spent so much time in crowded quarters aboard ships that he was ready to enjoy some privacy.

"This is the place for me, all right," John said with a satisfied sigh.

But even as his old ship was sailing away, John began to suspect that things might not be as perfect as they seemed. The trader was not too bad, but his African wife really frightened John. It was obvious from the start that she hated him, though John never could figure out why. Still, John was confident that he would prove to both the slave trader and his wife that he could make his own way and be successful in the slave trade business either with or without their help.

Then something happened that changed everything. Early one morning John awoke with a terrible headache and a raging fever. He felt so bad that he couldn't even get out of bed. When John didn't show up for breakfast the trader and his wife went to see about him. It took only one look for the trader to realize how seriously ill John was.

"He'll probably die," the trader said to his wife. "With these African diseases, who can tell? But for now you'll have to take care of him."

Although the woman was not at all happy about being given that responsibility, she did as she was told. But when, instead of getting better, John grew worse and worse, she gave up and totally ignored him. Even though John was burning up with fever, she wouldn't give him so much as a drink of cold water.

"Why should I waste my time nursing a dead man?" she asked with a shrug.

John's bed was nothing more than a grass mat

spread out on the ground. His pillow was a log of wood. And it was here that he lay day after day, moaning in misery and pain. His only help came from an occasional slave who took pity on him and brought him water and a bit of food.

But to everyone's amazement, John survived his illness. His fever disappeared as suddenly as it had come, and slowly he began to recover.

When the slaves told the woman about John's miraculous recovery, she was furious. "I don't know how he managed to do it," she exclaimed, "but before I'm finished with him he'll wish that he *was* dead."

It had been a long time since John had eaten much of anything, and he was terribly hungry. The woman knew that, but she would allow the slaves to give him only enough food to keep him from starving to death. To make it worse, she would have her table set up in a place where John couldn't help but see and smell the plates of delicious food that were served to her. And all the time she was eating she would make such remarks as, "Mmmmmmm! How tender this chicken is! Oh, what a delightful dessert! This is so wonderfully delicious! Give me more, give me more!" How John longed for some of that food from her table.

Had the slave trader been around, his wife would never have dared to treat John in such a cruel manner. But as it happened, he was off on a long trip to a distant island. That left John completely at the mercy of this cruel, vengeful woman. Even after he had completely recovered from the fever, he was kept weak and feeble through starvation.

Sometimes when the woman was in an especially good mood, she would allow John to have the scraps that were left on her plate when she was finished eating. Poor John was so hungry that he gratefully gobbled up every last crumb.

"John," she called out one day after she had finished her noon meal. "If you want to eat, you'll have to come and get my plate. There are some scraps left on it."

John quickly scrambled over to her table and grabbed the plate before she had a chance to change her mind. But his hands were shaking so badly that he dropped the plate and it shattered on the ground. Immediately John fell to his knees, trying to pick out the scraps of leftover food from among the pieces of broken pottery.

When the African woman saw John scratching for those few pitiful crumbs, she broke out laughing. Her laughter grew louder and louder and more and more cruel.

"Why, you're a dog, John Newton," she taunted. "You're just a skinny pet dog! I wonder if I could teach you some tricks?"

"Please, madam, can't I have some more to eat?" John begged. He was staring at her table, which was still laden with all kinds of delicious food.

"Absolutely not!" answered the woman.

By now John was frantic. "Please, *please!*" He cried. "Look at all the food you have left. What would it hurt if I just had a little?"

Every trace of laughter disappeared from the woman's face, and her voice grew sharp and cruel. "I said no, and I meant no! Now get away from my table. I'm tired of looking at you." Then, turning to her slaves she ordered, "Clear this table. Gather up all of the leftover food and throw it to the pigs. Not one crumb is to go to John Newton!"

Poor John had no choice but to drag his starving body back to his sleeping mat. There he lay for the rest of the day. Late that night, when everyone else was sleeping, John sneaked out and dug up some wild roots. He wiped the dirt off with his shirt, then he ate them skin and all. They tasted awful, and they were so tough that he could hardly bite into them. But in the months to come those raw roots were to make up the greatest part of John's diet.

"Wake up, John Newton! Wake up this minute!"

John opened his eyes to see the woman standing beside his mat.

"Get up, you lazy, worthless worm!" she screamed in a sudden fury.

John struggled to rise, but he was so weak that he could hardly manage it.

"Get up! Get up and walk!" she ordered.

Though it took every bit of strength he could muster, John finally made it to his feet. Limping badly, he walked a few steps, then he fell to his knees.

"Look at me! I'm John Newton!" One of the woman's slaves limped around mimicking John's halting steps. The woman laughed loudly and clapped her hands at the performance. When they saw her approval, the other slaves joined in, cheering loudly.

John hung his head. Hot tears of shame burned in his eyes.

"I never realized what a clown John Newton is!" the woman called out. "We really ought to reward him for his good performance by throwing coins, but we have no coins. What can we throw instead?"

"There are limes all over the ground," suggested someone. "Let's throw them."

"Good idea!" the woman answered. "Come on, everyone. Show your appreciation to the clown! Throw limes!"

John, still on his knees, cowered as the limes came flying through the air. The rotten ones splattered as they hit him, but the green ones were hard, and they really hurt. John tried to protect himself by covering his head with his arms, but it did little good. When they ran out of limes, the slaves picked up rocks and threw them. The woman stood back watching the scene and she roared with laughter.

That terrible torment continued day after day and week after week. None of the slaves dared to risk displeasing the cruel woman. They certainly didn't want her wrath to turn against them. But when she wasn't around, their scorn and ridicule toward John turned to pity. There were even those who occasionally dared to sneak him a little food from their own meager food allowance.

Finally the day came when the slave trader returned home. For John it was a day of rejoicing. At long last there was a ray of hope. John hurried to meet the trader, and he fell at his boss's feet. There he poured out the stories of his great suffering and torment at the hands of the man's wife.

"I can't believe that this is all true!" exclaimed the slave trader. "If my wife has treated you badly, I'm sure it's because you deserved it." Turning to his wife he asked, "Is this man telling me the truth, my dear?"

"Of course not!" she lied. "Who are you going to believe, this wretched man or me, your own wife?"

"Why, certainly I am going to believe you, dearest," the trader said quickly. Still, he couldn't help but notice that John was terribly weak and that he looked half starved. So he said to John, "We'll have to build up your health. I want you to go along on my next voyage. Maybe you'll finally be of some help to me."

The slave trader was true to his word. When he left on his next trip, John was with him.

And for a while things went fairly well. Then at one port John was accused by a drunken sailor of stealing from the trader. John was innocent of the charge, and he tried to explain what had really happened, but the slave trader wouldn't listen. He had already made up his mind that John was guilty.

"You had the nerve to accuse my wife of unfair cruelty?" he shouted angrily. "And now look at what has happened. You turn right around and rob me. Just you wait until we get back home! You'll learn what real suffering is."

For the rest of the trip, whenever the trader went ashore, he locked John to the ship's railing. John was given an allotment of one bowl of rice, which had to last him until the trader returned—even if it was several days. John would surely have starved to death had he not been able to catch a few fish from time to time.

The lack of food was only one of John's worries. Another was the weather. By now the rainy season had started. Since he was often locked up on deck, John had no choice but to sit there night and day. He had only a thin shirt and a pair of trousers to wear, and there was no shelter at all from the pouring rain and the freezing wind. It's no wonder that John was soon sick again.

When John and the slave trader arrived back at the island, things did not improve one bit. John was the most cruelly treated of all the slaves. And his terrible suffering was made even worse by the shame and helplessness he felt. He was allowed to own only one shirt and one pair of trousers, which he was not even permitted to wash. Sometimes late at night, when he was sure that the others were sleeping, he would sneak down to the ocean and quietly bathe with his clothes on. Then he would hurry back and go to sleep soaking wet, hoping that his clothes would be dry by morning. If they weren't he knew that he was in for another beating.

"Get up!" the slave trader called to John early one morning. "I have a big job for you to do today. I want a new lemon grove planted."

The sun was scorching hot, the work was terribly hard, and John was in such poor shape that it took great effort for him to even stand up. But he was ordered to get busy immediately digging holes and planting seedling trees. The job took John several days. Just as he was finishing, the slave trader and his wife came by to examine his work.

"Maybe by the time these trees grow up and bear fruit you will have gone back home to England and gotten a ship of your own," the slave trader said in a mocking voice. "Then you can come back here and help yourself to lemons." Turning to his wife he asked, "Do you think that's possible, my dear?"

"Possible?" she replied sarcastically. "Why, anything is possible. We see all kinds of strange things happen out here, don't we?"

John said nothing. He continued with his work, trying to ignore their sarcasm.

Soon the trader and his wife grew tired of their game and they walked away, laughing heartily.

John Newton was no longer the loud, boisterous, rude young man he had been when he first arrived at the African island. The fire was gone out of him. He had become helpless and terrified, able to do nothing but cower in fear before his tormentors.

Very often slave ships stopped at the island, but whenever John saw one coming, he ran off and hid himself among the palm trees. He was too ashamed to let anyone see his wretched condition.

Time and time again he thought about killing himself to escape his awful misery. But then he would think of Mary. It was only his memories of her and his great desire to get back to London to see her again that kept him alive.

Perhaps it was God's intention to humble John and to break his stubborn will. If so, it certainly looked as if He had succeeded.

10

Rescue at Last

When John's father retired from the sea and settled down in London, he began to think more and more about his son. It had been so long since he had received any word from John, and he was getting worried. Finally he decided that he would go and see a good friend of his—the owner of several merchant ships.

"I'm so worried about John," Mr. Newton told his friend. "I have no idea where he is or what might have happened to him. I realize that he has made a lot of trouble for himself in the past, but no one seems to have any idea where he is now."

"I've heard nothing about him," replied the man. "But I'll tell you what I'll do. Two of my trade ships are getting ready to leave London this week. One is headed for Italy and the other is going to Africa, but both of them will be stopping in many ports along the way. I'll give my captains orders to watch for your son. They can make inquiries in every port."

"Oh, thank you!" exclaimed Mr. Newton. "But

please, one more thing. If they should happen to find John, would you please tell them to bring him back here to London?"

"I'm sure that they'll do whatever they can," his friend answered.

So it was that when the two merchant ships sailed from London harbor, it was with direct orders to search for John Newton and, if possible, to bring him home on their return trip.

But on the African island, John's fortunes had changed considerably. He had been indescribably miserable with the slave trader and his wife, but the fact was that the trader was growing increasingly tired of John too.

"He's more trouble than he's worth," the man told his wife in disgust. "I thought that he would be a good addition to our group of slaves, but he's hardly able to do anything. I'm tired of seeing him around here."

"I'm tired of him, too," said his wife. "No matter what I do to him, he won't fight back. That man has absolutely no spirit at all."

Now, it so happened that John overheard the two of them talking. It gave him an idea, the first flicker of hope he had had in a long time. It just could be that this was his chance to get away from these awful people! This possibility gave John the courage to approach them.

"A merchant on the other side of this island is willing to have me go live with him if you'll permit it," John said nervously. "If you'll let me go, I'll be out of your way forever. I promise that I'll never bother you again."

The man and his wife just stared at John in silence. Falling to his knees, John begged, "Please let me go! Oh, please, please!"

"He's disgusting!" said the slave trader's wife. "I say we should let him go and good riddance!"

"Leave, then!" the slave trader ordered, punctuating his words with a sharp kick to John's ribs. "You've been nothing but a plague to us from the day you first arrived."

What a wonderful day that was for John! You can be sure he wasted no time in getting away! He had nothing to pack, because the only possessions he had left were the ragged clothes on his back.

When John arrived at the merchant's house, he was warmly welcomed. He was given new clothes to wear and all the food he could eat. With good care and the renewed hope it brought, John grew stronger and stronger every day. And because of his great gratitude to the merchant, John worked hard for him.

One day the merchant called John to him and said, "I'm very pleased with you, my boy. You work hard, and you're honest and responsible. I'm going to put you in charge of all my other servants here."

It wasn't long before John had proved himself to be a very capable manager, and his boss was greatly impressed. Again the merchant called John to him. "You are a good man, John Newton," he said. "Now I have another responsibility to add to your job."

"What is that, sir?" John asked.

"I want to put you in charge of all my money," his boss answered.

What a pleasant change that was for John. It certainly did feel good to finally be trusted and respected again!

Before long, John was sent to another island to take over the management of the merchant's trading business over there. Several other white servants lived on that island, and John was invited to move into their house with them. Soon John became very close friends with a red-haired Scotsman by the name of Will. Although Will was about fifty years old, the two of them enjoyed each other greatly. They were able to do as they pleased as long as their business showed a good profit. They enjoyed their life on the island. As for the merchant, he was more than satisfied, for under John's excellent management the business was doing extremely well.

"Not too long ago there was nothing in the world I wanted more than to get away from Africa forever. All I could think about day and night was going back to England," John told Will one evening as the two of them sat together on the front porch.

It was a beautiful night, warm with just the hint of a cool breeze. The only sound to be heard was the soft splashing of the waves as they broke gently upon the white sand.

After a long pause John continued, "But now—well, I'm not so sure that I would leave here even if I could."

"That's not so strange," Will answered. "I've seen that happen to many white men. Why, look at me! I've been here for almost thirty years! After living in Africa for a long time, a person seems to almost become an African . After a while he gets to where he likes Africa better than he likes his own country."

"Well, I guess it's just as well," John said with a sigh. "Even if I did get back to England, I don't imagine Mary would let me see her again. Did I ever tell you that I once asked her parents for permission to marry her? That was probably one of the stupidest things I've ever done."

"What's Mary like?" asked Will.

"I don't want to talk about her!" John said sharply.

Will should have known better than to press John for details about Mary. Thinking about her always made him moody. In an effort to change the subject Will asked, "When are you leaving on your trip inland?"

"I should've left last week," John said, "but I was hoping to get a few more things to trade. Let's try to flag down a passing ship tomorrow and see if we can buy some things. But even if I can't, I'd better leave early the following morning."

"Ships hardly ever come by this part of the coast," said Will. "You know that. Why waste time looking for them?"

"It won't hurt to walk along the beach for a little while," John said. "If we happen to see a ship, we'll signal it."

"In all the times we've walked down there, how often have we seen a trade ship pass by close enough to signal?" Will asked.

"Never," John admitted. "But there's always a first time. Anyway, it will give us some time to talk. After all, I'm going to be gone for almost five months!"

"Oh, all right." Will laughed. "We'll walk along the beach and watch for ships if that's what you want to do."

It was almost noon by the time John and Will got down to the beach. When they had been walking for almost two hours, Will suddenly exclaimed, "Look out there, John! There really is a ship! I can't believe it!"

"Let's make a fire and see if we can signal it," John said.

But by the time the fire was built and there was enough smoke to send the usual signal for trade, the ship had already sailed past.

"It's no use," said Will. "They won't be able to see the signal now."

"We've gone this far so we may as well try," John said. "The canoe isn't far from here. If the ship should stop, you can go out and see what kind of trade goods they have to sell. I'd better go on back and finish my packing for tomorrow."

After half an hour of signaling, Will declared, "This is useless! I'm going to put this fire out and go help John pack." He smothered the fire with sand and turned for one last look at the departing ship. But to his surprise, it was no farther away than when he first decided to put out the fire. Could it be that the ship had actually seen his signal and dropped anchor? He stood staring for a few more minutes. It was true! The ship wasn't moving!

Will ran to get the canoe. He carried it to the water and paddled out to where the ship was anchored.

When he climbed aboard, Will was greeted by the ship's captain himself. But before he had a chance to inquire about trade goods the captain asked, "Have you by any chance seen a man by the name of John Newton?"

"John Newton?" Will asked in surprise. "Yes, sir. I know him well. Why do you ask?"

"I have orders to find him and to bring him back to London," the captain replied. "Do you know where he is?"

"Yes. He's on shore getting ready to make a trip inland," Will answered. "He's leaving early tomorrow morning and won't be back for months."

"Then I'd better come ashore and deliver my message to him immediately," said the captain.

John was amazed to see Will walking up the beach with the ship's captain. He hurried out to meet him.

"So you're John Newton!" said the captain as he greeted John. "I'm so glad to have found you!" Then he told John all about his father's concern and his desire to have him back home.

When the captain finished talking, John turned and, without a word, walked slowly up the beach.

"John!" called the captain. "I need an answer from you! Are you coming with me, or aren't you?"

John turned and watched as the captain ran to catch up with him. "I don't know," John said slowly. "I just don't know. If you had come six months ago when I was a starving slave, I would have welcomed your offer as if you were going to bring me back from the dead. But things are different now, and to be honest, I'm not at all sure that I'd fit in with English life anymore. This is the happiest I've been in a long time—much better than my miserable life as a sailor!"

"If you come back with me, you'll share my cabin and eat at my table," the captain promised. "I won't expect you to do any work. Why should you? I already have all the sailors I need. Your only job will be to keep me company."

"You know, John," said Will, "even though you are far better off than you were when you lived with the slave trader, you still aren't a free man. You are, after all, nothing but a servant."

John said nothing. There were so many thoughts flooding his mind. Perhaps he should go back. He might never get another chance. Still, who knew what troubles and disasters might be awaiting him if he were to leave?

"John," said Will quietly, "what about Mary? Have you forgotten her?"

Forgotten Mary? Impossible! John could never forget Mary! But Will had said just the right thing. It was the memory of her that finally jarred John's thoughts into place. He would be a fool to let this opportunity pass him by!

"I'll go!" John announced. "When do we sail?"

The captain, smiling broadly, put his arm around John's shoulders. "Right away, my boy," he said. "Right away!"

11

The Long Trip Back

"I'm going home!" John exclaimed happily as the merchant ship sailed away from the coast of Africa. "I can hardly believe it. After all this time, I'm actually going home."

"We've got a long, long trip ahead of us, John," said the captain. "It takes a lot longer to gather up a shipload of merchandise for trade than to simply load up with a cargo of slaves, you know. In order to collect the gold, ivory, beeswax, and rare woods that we need, we'll have to make stops in the ports of many different countries."

"How long do you think this trip will take?" John asked.

"We've already been out for six months," the captain answered, "and I don't expect to be back for another year."

"I can hardly wait to see my father and Mary again," said John, "but as long as I know that we'll eventually end up in England, I won't complain."

Day after day after day went by, each one like the other. The port cities were interesting enough, but in between were long weeks at sea, and they stretched out endlessly. Since he wasn't working as a sailor, there was very little for John to do. He had hoped to use his time reading. He especially enjoyed books about math or tales of exciting adventures. But to his great disappointment there was only one book on board—*The Imitation of Christ.* It was all about the life of Jesus and what it meant to be His follower. There could not possibly have been a subject of less interest to John, but since there was nothing else to do, he reluctantly took the book to his cabin and began to read. Before the trip was over, he had read it through three times.

But once again John began to slip back into his old ways. It seemed that he could not say one single sentence without cursing the name of Jesus. And all the time he was getting into more and more trouble.

"I've heard stories about you, John," the captain said one day, "but I just couldn't believe that they were true. I didn't think it was possible for any person to be as bad a troublemaker as you were supposed to be. But now I'm not so sure. Can it possibly be that every one of those stories is true?"

"So you've heard stories about me, have you?" John laughed. "Well, you just listen to some stories I have to tell. And believe me, these are all true!" With that John started bragging about his many adventures, his near disasters, and all the trouble he had caused.

Although John had done just about everything a person could do to get into trouble, he had never joined the other sailors in drinking liquor, and he had never gotten drunk. But one night when he was especially bored, three sailors came up to him.

"We're challenging you to a drinking contest," said one sailor.

"I don't like liquor," John replied.

"I doubt that!" sneered another. "I think it's just that you know that we'll have to sneak into the captain's cabin to steal the liquor, and you're afraid that you'll get caught and get into trouble!"

"Afraid? Who, me?" John laughed. "You should know by now that I'm not afraid of anything, especially not of the captain!"

"Oh?" said the third sailor. "Well, I say that you're afraid to join us!"

"I'm not afraid!" shouted John.

"Shhhhh!" warned the others. "Don't let the captain hear you!"

"I'm not afraid, and I'll prove it," said John. "Just give me a couple of minutes and I'll be back with enough rum to keep us going all night."

John was true to his word. When he returned, his arms were filled with stolen bottles.

"Let the bravest man begin!" challenged the first sailor.

"That's me!" called John. "Hand me a bottle!"

And so the drinking contest was under way. For every drink the other sailors took, John took two. Suddenly, as if a fire had been set inside of him, John jumped to his feet and began dancing around like a madman. The other sailors roared with laughter. "What a fool he is!" they cried. "What a stupid fool!"

Just then the wind blew John's hat off. It flew over the railing and into the water below. John stopped his dancing, felt his bare head, and stared at the others in confusion. "My hat's gone!" he cried. "Where did my hat go?"

"It blew into the ocean," a sailor laughed.

Before anyone could stop him, John jumped over the side of the ship. Now, even when he was sober John couldn't swim. Everyone knew that. The other sailors were too drunk to help him, and since it was past midnight everyone else was sleeping.

"He's gone," said one drunken sailor sadly.

"Yes, he's gone," agreed another. "That current is awfully strong. He's been swept away and drowned by now."

Suddenly there was a loud crashing, knocking noise, so loud that everyone on the ship was awakened. They jumped from their bunks and came running to see what all the noise was about.

"It seems to be coming from the side of the ship," called the first mate. He ran to the railing and peered over into the darkness. "Why, it's John Newton! Look, he's hanging on the side!"

Sure enough, it was John. He hadn't gone into the water at all, for his jacket had gotten snagged on a loose board. That board had saved his life.

Another time, while the ship was in port, several of the sailors decided to go into the woods and do some hunting. They shot an enormous water buffalo, big enough to give them fresh meat for weeks. The men packed up as much of the meat as they could carry, then they hid the rest of it in a cool, shady place and carefully marked the spot.

It was late afternoon before the hunting party was ready to go back into the woods to collect the rest of the meat. "I hope we can find our way," said one sailor doubtfully.

"Don't worry. I'll be the guide," John announced.

"Maybe we'd better wait until morning," someone suggested. "We sure don't want to be lost out there in the dark!"

"That's silly! I'm probably the best guide in all of Africa," John boasted. "I'll get you there and back again long before the sun sets."

The hunting party had been walking for over an hour when a sailor finally asked, "Are you sure you know where you're going, John? This doesn't seem right to me."

Without a moment's hestitation John answered, "Trust me! I know exactly where we are."

After another hour others began to complain. "We've been walking too long," said one.

"We aren't going to make it back before dark," said another.

"Quit complaining!" snapped John. "I said I'd get you there, and I will!"

But as the sun sank lower and lower in the western sky, even John had to admit that they were hopelessly lost.

"It's all your fault, John Newton!" one man accused. "You always think you know everything."

"Be quiet!" ordered John. "What good does it do to blame me? You'd better save your energy for helping us find our way out of here."

As the night grew darker, the band of men became more and more lost and confused. It was obvious to everyone that they were going deeper and deeper into the woods, but no one knew what to do. At one point they had to wade through a swamp with water almost up to their shoulders.

"Listen!" whispered one sailor. "What's that noise?"

"It's some wild animal," came the answer. "These woods are full of them."

The little party was in a very bad way, and every one of the men knew it. It was a dark, cloudy night, and they had no light at all. Nor did they have food, a compass, or weapons. Each one fully expected a tiger to pounce out and tear him to pieces at any moment.

"We're going to die, you know," whispered one man. "There's no way we'll ever make it out of here."

No one answered. Though they didn't want to say so, everyone was certain that the sailor was right.

Suddenly the clouds cleared and the moon rose, full and bright. By the light of the moon, the sailors struggled on until they made it to the shore and finally back to the ship. As they climbed aboard, weak with exhaustion and fear, a sailor mumbled, "It was God Himself who led us back. For some reason He wants us alive."

It was January 1748 when the ship finally turned around and headed back toward England. But their problems were far from over. Because the voyage had been so long and the weather so hot, the ship was in very poor condition. And the whole way home they were lashed by one storm after another.

"In all my years at sea I've never before seen a

voyage so plagued with trouble," said the captain. "I think it's all your fault, John Newton. You're a curse to any ship you're on. You're just like Jonah! And I should have done exactly what Jonah's captain did—I should have thrown you overboard!"

12

Welcome Home!

When at long last the trading ship docked at London Harbor, Mr. Newton was standing on the wharf waiting to welcome his son home. John walked down the gangplank and out onto the pier. For several minutes he and his father stood perfectly still, staring at each other in awkward silence. Neither one seemed to know what to do next.

It was Mr. Newton who finally stepped forward. Throwing his arms around his son he cried, "Oh, John, I've been so worried about you! Last week I heard that this ship was due in port any day. Since then I've spent every minute down here waiting—hoping and praying that the captain had found you and you would be on board. Now here you are. My prayers were answered."

That night, sitting in the warmth of his father's house, John talked about his many adventures. He told of his escape from the hated man-of-war and of the terrible punishments he had endured after his capture. He told of being traded to the slave ship and how he himself had been forced to live as a slave on the African Island. Then he told about his release to the merchant and how happy his time had been with him.

"I couldn't believe it when my friend and I saw a trade ship sailing so close to our coast," John continued. "Then when I saw the captain walking up the beach with Will, I didn't know what to think. And when he said that he was under orders to find me and bring me home—well, I just can't tell you how amazed I was. The one ship to ever come by that close to shore just happened to be the one ship that was searching for me. Can you imagine such great luck as that?"

"It wasn't luck at all," said John's father.

"What do you mean?" asked John in surprise. "Of couse it was luck. It was wonderfully good luck."

"No, it wasn't," answered his father firmly. "What it was was God. He was the one who caused the ship to pass by at just the right time. God sent that ship to bring you back home, John."

For a long while John sat in silence watching the bright flames dancing in the fireplace. When he finally spoke, it was slowly and thoughtfully.

"Father, I don't want to hurt you," he said, "but I think you need to understand something about me. I'm no longer the little boy who went to sea with you so many years ago. I'm grown up now, and I have ideas of my own and my own way of doing things. To my way of thinking, there really isn't any reason to believe in God. If He does exist—which I doubt—then He obviously cares nothing about me. Now you tell me, Father, why should I have any interest in knowing God?"

"I know all about your way of doing things, John," said his father sadly. "Sailors everywhere are talking about John Newton. They say that you are the proudest of the proud and the most stubborn of the stubborn. They say you are a liar, a thief, and a troublemaker. They say you are the worst curse that can befall any ship. I don't know how many of the stories I hear about you are really true. Surely not all of them. No one could do all the things they say you've done. Still, there must be a certain amount of truth in them." Then with great sadness in his eyes he looked straight at John and said, "Son, I just can't understand this change in you."

"You can't understand it?" asked John bitterly. "Then let me explain it to you. After a lot of pain and suffering I finally came to realize that my prayers were not being answered. And what's more, they were not going to be answered. It was quite obvious that there was no one watching out for me. If I was going to make it at all, I would have to do it on my own. Now everything I do is done my own way, to help me, and to make me happy. And I'll tell you something else—there will be trouble for anyone who gets in my way. I won't take orders from anyone."

Mr. Newton stared in dismay at this angry young man with the sneering mouth and flashing eyes. In a quiet voice he asked, "And how has it worked out doing everything your own way, John?"

"Not too well," John admitted. But he quickly added, "Things will be going a lot better now, though. Have you heard what I'm going to be doing?"

"I thought you would be staying here in London," said Mr. Newton in surprise.

"Oh, no! I'm going to be the captain of a ship," John announced proudly.

"Really?" asked his father. "What kind of a ship is it?"

"It's a slave ship," answered John. "That's where the money is, you know." He leaned back in his chair and added with a satisfied sigh, "No more bosses for me, Father. And no more orders—except for the ones I give, of course. My problems are finally over."

The next day John went to see Mary Catlett. "I'm not going to stay long," he assured her parents. "I just wanted to come by and see how you all are doing."

"We're just fine," said Mary excitedly. "But you must stay and tell us about everything that's happened to you since we saw you last."

So John repeated the tales of his many adventures. This time, though, he left out the part about his terror and humiliation at the hands of the slave trader and his African wife. He couldn't bear to have Mary know about that disgraceful situation.

"What an exciting life you've had!" exclaimed Mary's sister. "I can hardly believe that one person could have had so many adventures and narrow escapes."

"You haven't heard half of them," John boasted. "I've had some awfully hard times in my life, but I must admit that I've also had more than my share of unexpected good luck."

"It sounds as if you've had a lot more than just luck, my boy," said Mr. Catlett. "It sounds to me as if God Himself has taken great pains to preserve your life."

"It certainly does," agreed Mrs. Catlett. "And you know, John, it's a fact that when God miraculously spares a person's life—as He obviously has yours—that it's usually because He has a very special purpose for that person. I wonder what plans He might have for you."

"I don't know anything about God's plans for me." John laughed. "But I sure do know what my plans are. And to my way of thinking, it's my plans that are the important ones!"

John proceeded to tell the Catletts all about his new slave ship. "Isn't it exciting?" he asked when he had finished. "At last I'm going to get the chance to be the captain of a ship."

Mary, however, was not nearly as excited as John was. "Do you really have to go back to sea, John?" she asked sadly. "Maybe the life of a sailor really isn't the best life for you."

"Of course I don't have to go back to sea," John answered. "But that's what I want to do, so that's what I will do." John hadn't intended to speak so sharply to Mary. In a more gentle voice he added. "A sailor is what I am, Mary. Can't you see that this is my big chance? Being a captain—the boss of a ship—is every sailor's dream. I was afraid that I'd never get this chance, and now here it is. I just can't let it pass me by. You can understand that, can't you?"

"But why does it have to be a slave ship?" Mary asked.

"There's nothing wrong with a slave ship," said John. "One kind of cargo is no different than another—except that with slaves the voyages are shorter and I'll get paid more. Why should I complain about that?"

"Well," said Mary with a sigh, "God did answer my prayers. He brought you back safely. And I'm sure that He will also watch over you on the slave ship. Now I'll just have to trust Him to hear and answer my other prayer for you."

"And just what might that other prayer be?" asked John with a smile.

"It's my greatest prayer of all, John," Mary answered softly. "It's that you will come to love God and that you will ask Jesus Christ to be your Savior."

"I'll be leaving London soon," John said abruptly. "We won't have very much time together. Please, let's not waste the little time we do have talking about God!"

13

Kill Those Rebels!

For the next six years, Captain John Newton sailed between Africa and the slave markets of the world. Whenever his travels took him to London, John made arrangements to stay for an extra day or two. He enjoyed seeing his father and bragging about how well he was doing. But it was the time he spent with Mary that he enjoyed the most.

"I'll marry her some day," John told his father, "but not until I'm rich enough to buy her the best of everything."

But wealth was not the thing that concerned Mary. What concerned her was John's attitude toward God. Nothing she said or did could change his hatred, his disbelief, and his anger toward God.

Nor was there any change in John's undisciplined behavior. And since he was now the captain of the ship, his actions influenced all of the crewmen on board. It wasn't long before John Newton's ship became known as the wildest, dirtiest slave ship to sail the seas. John was mercilessly cruel to the African captives who were unfortunate enough to be loaded onto his ship, and he didn't treat his crew much better.

"It isn't wise to make enemies of everyone," the first mate once warned John. "Everybody needs to have some friends."

"What's that supposed to mean?" John asked irritably. "I've got plenty of friends."

"Like who?" the first mate asked. "I'll bet there isn't one single man on board who considers himself a friend of yours."

"What business is it of yours anyway?" John snapped. "A captain doesn't need friends. I'm the boss around here, you know. The men will do whatever I tell them to do whether they like it or not. If they don't, they'll pay the price for disobeying me."

Very early one morning—on a particularly long, hot trip from Africa to England—a crewman suddenly burst through John's cabin door.

"The Africans are rebelling!" he cried. "They've started to fight us!"

Now, this was a terrifying situation indeed. In fact, it was the very worst situation that could possibly happen on a slave ship. There were so many more African captives aboard than there were crewmen. Every sailor had heard horrifying stories about rebellions where the Africans had succeeded in taking over the ship and then had thrown the crewmen overboard to drown.

Jumping from his bunk John commanded, "Bolt the doors! Don't let them get up onto the deck!"

"We have bolted the doors, sir," the crewman answered. "but it's too late! The deck is already swarming with slaves!"

There was not a moment to lose. Pushing the crewman aside, John ran out onto the deck to see how bad the situation really was. Immediately he was surrounded by the angry mob of black men. Their legs still bound in chains, they lunged at him, shouting words he could not understand and shaking their fists menacingly.

"Get the whips!" John ordered.

Within minutes the huge leather whips were cracking through the air, lashing into the mob of rebels and driving them back. For a while it looked as if this would work. The Africans were being forced back down below deck. But even the whips could not hold the men back for long. There were just too many of them. With a roar of hatred and rage they surged forward, grabbing at the whips, trying to get them away from the sailors.

"Captain!" yelled the first mate. "If they get the whips, they will use them against us! That's what happened to Captain Simmons, remember, and no one but the cabin boy survived that uprising!"

"Get the guns!" John commanded. "Shoot every black man on this deck! And if we have to, we'll kill every African man, woman, and child down in the hold too!"

That was the command the sailors had been waiting for. They lost no time in following their captain's orders. The chained captives were no match for the smoking firearms of the desperate crewmen. Before long, not a single black man was alive on the deck. The uprising had been crushed.

With the door to the hold of the ship securely bolted, John walked around the deck inspecting the damage. The sails were badly ripped, and the masts were almost destroyed. Portions of the railing were completely torn away, and gaping holes had been blown in the deck. And lying everywhere were the bodies of the African men who had died in this last attempt to regain their freedom.

"Throw them overboard!" John commanded coldly. "And I want every one of those Africans down below to be punished. They are to have no food today or tomorrow, and only half of their usual food allotment for the rest of the trip. Except for the time it takes you to throw food down, I don't want that door unbolted for a single minute until we are safely docked in England!"

John Newton stood by, watching with satisfaction as the bodies of the dead Africans were thrown overboard. He was feeling extremely pleased with himself. After all, the worst of all possible situations had occurred and he had handled the emergency quickly, efficiently, and thoroughly.

"It surely is too bad," said the first mate shaking his head sadly.

"What's too bad?" asked John.

"That all those men had to die for nothing," the first mate answered.

"Hah!" said John bitterly. "There's only one thing that's too bad, and that's that I'll get so little money for this wretched load of slaves. All I've got left is half a load of women and children, and I don't know how many of them will still be alive when we get to England. Now *that's* too bad!"

14

Captain John

That night John lay in his bunk unable to sleep. Hour after hour dragged by as he tossed and turned, staring out into the darkness. If only he could stop all those memories from crowding his mind!

"My life has been one long tragedy!" John exclaimed aloud. "Just one miserable catastrophe after another!"

The memories that were troubling John the most were of the terrible time he had spent as a prisoner of the slave trader. It was with great bitterness that he remembered his awful suffering, his gnawing hunger and paralyzing fear, his humiliation and despair so great that it drove him to the very brink of suicide. Worst of all was the horrible, degrading cruelty of the slave trader's African wife. It was those memories that flooded John's soul with a seething, burning hatred.

It would seem that the memory of his own captivity would cause John to feel compassion and pity for the poor, helpless slaves who lay chained together below the deck of his ship. But it didn't. Instead, it caused his hatred for the Africans to grow even greater.

"There will never again be an African uprising on my ship!" John resolved. "From now on I'll pack them in so tightly that they won't be able to move. And I'll give them so little food and water that they'll be too weak to even think about fighting."

John was determined to live up to that resolution. It seemed as though he poured out upon the captives all of the pain and anger and hatred he felt for the cruel African woman.

"If you treat the slaves so roughly and if you continue to starve them like you're doing, it really punishes you as much as it punishes them," one of the officers explained to John one day. "So many of them die. The ones who manage to survive are so weak and sickly and scrawny when they arrive at the slave market that you either have to spend months getting them ready to sell or else you sell them as they are and end up getting paid almost nothing for your trouble. Either way you lose."

"What's it to you?" John snapped. "You get your pay, don't you? The captives on my ship are my property, and I'll treat them any way I want to."

But the officer's observations must have made some sense to John—even though he wouldn't admit it—because he did order immediate increases in the Africans' food allowance. He even eased up a bit on the harsh treatment they received.

As conditions improved for the captives, however, they got steadily worse for the crewmen. John seemed to be turning his hateful wrath toward them. He treated the sailors more unfairly and with more cruelty every day, and every day the sailors hated him more. Before long, whispered threats against his life were circulating around the ship.

"If we were to kill the captain and take over the ship, no one would blame us one bit," whispered one angry crewman to a group of sailors.

"We could certainly do a better job of running it than he is doing," added another.

"We've been talking this way for a long time," said a third, "but our talk is getting us nowhere. When are we going to do something about it?"

"Tomorrow, I say!" said the first sailor. "Let's get rid of the captain tomorrow!"

"If we are really going to do it, we had better do it right," cautioned an older sailor. "We'll get no second chance."

"We need to make careful plans," added someone. "And we need to have a leader. I think it should be you, Henry."

"Aye, aye!" several others chimed in.

"Any objections?" the sailor asked. When no one spoke up he said, "Then it's settled. You tell us what to do, Henry, and we'll do it."

"Well, I do have an idea," said Henry.

And so, long into the night, the little group sat together quietly working out a plan. When all of the details had been decided, Henry solemnly said, "You mates know that what we're proposing to do—kill the captain and take over the ship—is mutiny, don't you?"

"Aye," they all answered.

"And you do understand that every one of us could be put to death for participating in such a scheme?"

"Aye," came the answer again.

"If anyone wants to back out, I'll understand. But you must do it now if you're going to. Does anyone want out? If so, speak up."

Henry waited for several minutes, but no one said a word. "Then we're all in it together," he said. "Good! Now everyone go and get some sleep. Tomorrow will be a big day."

It wasn't two hours after the meeting ended that each of the sailors in the group was awakened by Henry's best friend, Ben. "Henry's terribly sick!" whispered Ben. "I don't know what's wrong with him. It came on so fast!"

"He must have caught one of those awful African diseases," someone suggested.

"I don't know, but the way he's going, it's unlikely that he'll live until morning," Ben continued. "If we're serious about going through with our plan to kill the captain tomorrow we had better choose a new leader."

"How about you, Ben?" one sailor asked. "Does everyone agree to Ben for our new leader?"

"Aye!" answered the rest.

"OK, I'll do it," said Ben. "We'll keep the same plan. But be careful. Don't anyone do anything until you get the signal from me. Now let's get back to bed before someone gets suspicious."

The next morning the men were up early and busy at their chores. They carefully avoided each other, hardly even speaking for fear of raising suspicion. But each one kept his eyes on Ben, always watching for the signal that would set their plan in motion.

Suddenly, with no warning at all, an enormous wave crashed against the side of the ship and swept over the deck.

"Man overboard! Man overboard!" shouted the first mate. "It's Ben! He was washed overboard!"

Although they searched frantically for hours, Ben was never found. "I've never seen anything like it!" the first mate exclaimed, shaking his head in wonder. "It's as if that wave came out of nowhere and swept Ben completely off the face of the earth."

The conspiring group of sailors glanced around at each other. They were terrified. As soon as they were able to get away from the others, they quickly assembled in the privacy of a back storeroom. "Henry and Ben are both gone! Two leaders dead in just a matter of hours!" exclaimed one. "What do you mates make of it?"

"I think it's a sign to us," said one in a nervous whisper.

"Yes," agreed another. "For some reason God wants the captain alive, and He's punishing us for plotting against him."

Then a third sailor said, "If we go through with our plan, we'll all die."

And so, though the sailors continued to hate and fear Captain John Newton, there was no more talk of mutiny.

15

The Ship Is Sinking

It was just past midnight on March 21, 1748. Twenty-three-year-old John Newton, slave ship captain, was sound asleep in his cabin. Suddenly a huge wave crashed against the wooden ship, knocking it to one side. John was thrown out of his bunk and onto the floor, where he landed with a splash. To his alarm John saw that his cabin was quickly filling up with water!

Leaping up, John dashed out of his room, up the ladder, and onto the deck. As he ran he shouted, "All hands on deck! Sound the alarm! All hands on deck!"

"We're sinking, sir!" cried the frantic sailor who met him at the top of the ladder.

John turned to sound the alarm. When he turned back, the sailor was gone.

"He was washed overboard, sir!" gasped another sailor in disbelief. "He was standing right there one minute, and the next minute he was gone!"

"Don't take time to worry about him!" commanded John hoarsely. "Unless some miracle happens we will all be joining him at the bottom of the sea. The ship is filling up with water fast."

The violent storm had blown up so quickly that no one had any warning. Huge waves beat wildly against the ship, threatening to break it apart at any minute. The crewmen used heavy ropes to tie themselves to the ship's railing in an effort to keep from being washed overboard. Torrents of rain poured down hour after hour, and the thunder roared so loudly that the men had to yell in order to make themselves heard.

The pounding waves had torn away the upper timbers on one side of the deck, and the men watched helplessly as barrel after barrel of food and precious provisions washed overboard. Though everyone worked tirelessly, no one on board really expected to survive this deadly storm. Captain John Newton was working the pump full speed, but water poured into the ship faster than he could pump it out.

"You!" John shouted to a sailor nearby. "Get ten or twelve other men—anyone who isn't doing essential work—and get busy bailing this water out. Use buckets, pails, kettles—anything that will hold water."

But their efforts were in vain. The ship continued to fill with water faster than the men could bail it out. All of a sudden John felt as though he was an eleven-year-old boy again, terrified by his first storm at sea. He had been in many, many wild storms since then, but now John was filled with the same terrible panic and terror that he had felt that very first time.

"Father!" John cried out loud. "Father, help me!" But this time his father wasn't there. "The ship is going to sink and I can't swim!" he shouted frantically.

Then, lifting his face toward heaven, John cried out, "Please, God, help me! Don't let me die! Oh, God, I know what a terrible sinner I am. Surely there is not another man alive as evil as me. I know that I don't deserve Your mercy, but I'm begging You to please take pity on me. Forgive me for all the wicked things I've done, and I promise You that I'll be different from now on! Please, God, please have mercy on me and spare my life!"

And God, in His great love and mercy, heard John Newton's prayer. The storm began to ease just as suddenly as it had come. By noon the next day, after nine straight hours, John was finally able to leave the pump. The sea was once again calm and smooth.

The ship was badly damaged, but the crewmen were so exhausted that they didn't want to do anything except lie on the deck and rest. John, however, could see that water was already beginning to leak back into the battered ship.

"This is no time to rest!" John told them. "Gather up anything we can use to stop up these leaks—bedding, clothes, anything! We're turning around and heading back to England, and we'll have our hands full keeping this miserable wreck of a ship afloat until we get there."

The weather was bitterly cold, and the men shivered in their soaking wet shirts and trousers, but they had to use every bit of extra clothing to stop up the leaks. Every blanket was used, every towel, and every pillow. All of this was stuffed into the cracks and holes, and then pieces of wooden boards were nailed over them. When they saw how well the patches worked, the men finally allowed themselves to hope that maybe—just maybe—they actually did have a chance of making it back home after all.

Now that the immediate danger was over, John sank down on his bed, absolutely exhausted. But he did not go to sleep. He could not get this miraculous escape from certain death out of his mind. What had made him beg God for mercy? Why, he didn't even believe in God! Anyway, how could there ever be mercy for such a sinner as he? If God was just and fair—and that's what John had always been taught—then surely there could be no forgiveness for him.

John remembered his early Christian training at his mother's knees. He remembered the many warnings he had received and all of the times that his life had been spared. So often he had been given the opportunity to make a new start, but every time he had gone back to his wicked and sinful life. How much hatred he had carried toward God! Surely his sins were far too great to ever be forgiven! Still, it certainly did seem as though God had answered his prayer.

A consuming desire to know more about Jesus Christ, God's Son, whom he had cursed so often, flooded over John. Then he remembered the book he had read while he was on board the merchant ship coming back from his African captivity. In it he had read all the details of Jesus' life, His death, and His resurrection.

"Jesus didn't die for His own sins," John said aloud. "He was sinless. He died for those people who realize their own helplessness and are willing to put their trust in Him. People like me!"

That is what he had read, but how could he know for sure that it was all true?

There's so much I don't understand, John thought. *The only thing I can do is assume that the Bible is true and that God really can and will forgive my sins. I will believe it all until I find out otherwise.* It was with that comforting thought that John drifted off into a calm and restful sleep.

The next morning dawned clear and beautiful. The sea was calm and smooth, the breeze gentle. But very soon panic siezed the crew once again, for they discovered that almost everything had been washed overboard and lost at sea. It didn't matter that all of the water barrels were gone, because there was plenty of rainwater to drink. The big problem was that all of their food was also gone. There was nothing left on board to eat except a little grain that had been meant for the hogs. In order to survive they had to catch fish—by hand since their fishing gear was gone. The firewood had also been washed away, so the fish was eaten raw.

Even though the wind was good and the weather fair, the ship proceeded slowly because the sails had been blown to shreds. At first the navigator thought that the ship was only about a hundred leagues from England, but it had been blown so far off course that they were in fact much farther away. The pumps had to be manned constantly to keep the ship above water and the men were half frozen and half starved.

"You know what's going to happen, don't you?" one man moaned in despair. "After surviving all of this, we'll die just before we make it to land."

"Remember Captain White's ship?" said another. "They were in a situation very much like ours. They were starving, too. Before they were rescued they had resorted to eating each other."

Every day the men grew weaker, and their situation seemed more and more hopeless. On the tenth day a sailor died. Only John Newton was still convinced that they would make it to England alive.

"Why would God bring us this far if He didn't intend to rescue us?" he asked. "We musn't give up hope!"

As for John, he spent the endless days reading a Bible that one of the sailors had brought along and praying to God for mercy and forgiveness.

As dawn broke the morning of April 8, 1748, the crewmen were awakened by joyful shouts from the sailor who was standing watch on deck. "Land ho! I see land!" he cried. "We've made it! We're home!"

And it was on that day, eighteen days after the devastating storm, that the battered wreck of a slave ship limped into the harbor at Lough Swilly, Ireland. They had hardly dropped anchor and made it to shore when violent winds once again began to blow and the sea began to churn. The ragged, half-starved sailors watched in horror as their ship flopped over onto its side and sank to the bottom.

"Now I know for sure!" gasped John Newton. "There is a God above! And He does hear and answer prayer. Why, just look at how He answered mine!"

16

A New Man

"Won't you take me to London?" John begged every ship's captain he saw in Lough Swilly. "I must get there as quickly as possible. Please, can't anyone take me home?"

"Why are you in such a hurry?" asked an old, white-haired captain.

"Because I have to see my father," John replied. "I've put him through so much worry and despair. Now I want him to know that I've changed. I've become a new person."

"A new person?" the captain asked. "What do you mean by that?"

"I've just made a wonderful discovery!" John exclaimed. "I've found out what it means to have my sins forgiven by Jesus Christ. He changed my life and made me a child of God."

The captain smiled broadly at John's obvious sincerity and excitement. "Good for you, my boy!" he answered. "I know exactly what you're talking about. You see, I'm a Christian, too. If you don't mind my saying so, I've heard plenty of stories about you, John Newton, and not a one of them was good. I'm sure that this news will be the best gift you could ever give your father. It will make him very happy."

"If I could only get home to tell him about it," John said sadly.

"Well now, I just might be persuaded to take you there myself," said the captain.

"Really?" asked John in surprise. "But I thought you weren't going to London."

"I wasn't," replied the captain with a grin. "But it just occurred to me that I haven't seen London for quite a while. This seems like a pretty good time for me to do it, don't you think so?"

"Absolutely!" agreed John. "It's a perfect time!"

It took several days to get the ship ready, but the trip itself wasn't long. Just before they reached London the captain called John over to him.

"I'm afraid I have bad news for you," he said. "One of the crewmen knows your father well. He told me that your father was convinced that your ship had gone down in the storm and that you had been lost at sea. Your father was so sad and depressed that he decided to leave England for good. You just missed him, John. Not two days ago he left to take a government position in India."

Tears filled John's eyes. "I so wanted to spend some time with him," he said. "You can't imagine the sadness and pain I've caused him. I wanted to apologize for that, and then I wanted to ask him to help me. I need him to advise me and to teach me in the ways of Christianity. This whole thing is so new to me, you see."

"Perhaps he'll be back before long," said the captain gently. "You'll still have the chance to talk with him."

"I don't think so," John replied sadly. "I have a feeling that I'll never see my father again."

"Why don't you write to him, then?" suggested the captain. "You could tell him everything you told me."

"I'll do that!" answered John. "It won't be as good as talking to him, but it's better than nothing. At least he'll know I'm alive."

The captain was greatly attracted to John and was very much impressed by the young man's sincerity in his new faith. John's disappointment upon hearing that he had missed seeing his father touched the old man so deeply that he decided to help John as much as he possibly could. In the days that they were able to spend together, he encouraged him, taught him, advised him, and answered his endless questions.

"Do you know what really surprises me?" John asked the old man. "It seemed so obvious to me that it was the hand of God that was responsible for that storm—and also for our miraculous escape—yet no one else on the ship seemed to realize it. I just can't understand that."

"I can," answered the captain. "God wasn't talking to any of them. He was talking to you."

"Well, He sure got my attention," said John.

When John's new friend left to return to Ireland,

John went to the docks to bid him a grateful farewell. "I've known you for such a short time," John said, "but I feel like you are a second father to me. I'll never forget you."

"And I'll never forget you, John," the captain replied. "I'll pray for you every day."

"Do you think we'll ever see each other again?" John asked.

"I'm sure of it!" replied the captain. "Now you go and see that girlfriend of yours. Tell her about the change in you."

With that, the two friends parted, and John headed for Kent.

"Praise be to God!" Mary cried when John finished telling her all that had happened to him, "My prayers have been answered. God has spared your life and He has saved your soul."

"Yes," said John happily. "Praise be to God!"

"I suppose that after all you've been through you'll be staying in London now," Mary said hopefully.

"Oh, no!" John replied quickly. "I'm going to be the captain of another slave ship. Sailing is my whole life, Mary. You can understand that, can't you?"

"But John, surely you don't think that God wants you to continue selling slaves!" exclaimed Mary in surprise.

"Why not?" asked John. "I can't understand why you're so against the slave business. The Lord God has mercifully forgiven my sins, but that doesn't mean that He wants me to change my whole life, does it? Isn't it enough that I've promised Him that I would give up my sinful ways and become a better person?"

John Newton continued to sail his slave ship for six more years. He was a Christian, and He did love God, but—though it seems impossible—he hadn't the least feeling of pity or compassion for the miserable, terrified African captives who lay tightly packed and chained in the hold of his ship.

At first John seemed to have become a totally different person. His Bible was always with him when he went to sea, and he read it every day. He even held Christian services for the sailors on board his ship.

But very soon John found that his great resolutions were not as easy to keep as he had imagined. There was no one on board to encourage or instruct him, and Satan's temptations were great. John began to slip back into some of his old habits, though that made him feel guilty and ashamed.

In all of his many trips to and from the African continent, never since his rescue had John set foot upon the island where he had once lived as a slave. The idea of seeing the hated slave trader or his wife kept him as far away from that island as possible. But while he was in London, John was told that his old enemies had become so hated that they were finally driven away. That set John to thinking about the island and wondering how much it had changed. And so it was to that island that John's ship headed.

When the ship dropped anchor, John went ashore. He was absolutely amazed at the island's beauty and peacefulness. That was not at all the way he remembered it. But as he walked around this place that he had known so well and hated so much, painful memories came rushing back to him. Remembering the lemon grove he had been forced to plant, John walked to the clearing to see if the trees were still standing. He gasped in amazement when he saw the tall trees covered with lemons. Smiling bitterly, John picked a lemon, cut it open, and sucked its juice. How well he remembered the way the slave trader and his wife had ridiculed and mocked him about those trees.

"They joked about my coming back on a ship of my own and helping myself to these lemons," he said aloud. "And now look at me. That is exactly what has happened. Oh, how I wish those two were here! I would give anything to be able to laugh in their faces."

John was God's child, but he wasn't living like one. His desire for revenge was proof of that. Although he had gratefully accepted the total forgiveness that God had offered him, he was not willing to forgive anyone who had wronged him. So once again God found it necessary to get John's attention. That very night John became sick with a violent fever. For almost a week he suffered terribly, and there were times when his men were sure that he would die.

With shame and sorrow John recalled how God had repeatedly stretched out His merciful, loving hand to rescue him. He remembered his earnest prayers and all of his solemnn promises to God. He had tried hard to keep those promises, but in the end he had broken every single one of them. It was on the seventh day that John, weak and delirious, crawled from his bed and crept to a secluded part of the island. Once again he fell to his knees in anguished prayer.

"This time I'm not asking You to save my life, Lord," he prayed. "Perhaps I'm not even worth the trouble. And I'm not going to make You any more promises, either, because I know I can't keep them. There's only one thing I want to say to You. Please take my life and do whatever You want to do with it. I'm Your child, and I know that You will do what is best."

John struggled back to his bed and fell into a deep sleep. When he awoke the next morning he knew that everything would be fine. In two days his body was completely well, but something even greater had happened. The great weight of guilt he had carried for so long was finally gone.

Before the ship reached its destiny in Charleston, South Carolina, eight crewmen had died of the same fever that John had suffered. "No one survives it," said the first mate, shaking his head in wonder. "No one, that is, except you, Captain!"

"Whether I live or whether I die, I am in the hands of God," John replied softly.

The ship remained in Charleston for almost a month. Every day that they were there John went alone into the woods, his Bible under his arm. There he would read and pray, asking for guidance from the Lord. It was there in the woods, alone with the Lord, that John began to understand that God could never be pleased with a person who treated other human beings like animals. All men—whether black or white—were created in the image of God, and every single one of them was precious in His sight.

"Dear God," John prayed, "if I'm doing the wrong thing by running a slave ship, please show me. I'm willing to stop if that's what You want me to do."

17

No More Sailing

With his business in America completed, John Newton turned his ship toward England. It was a long way home, so he had a lot of time to think. Reflecting back on his wild, wasted life brought tears to John's eyes. How different it could have been had he allowed the Lord God to take control! And he thought about Mary, too. How he missed her. Had it not been for her prayers God might never have pursued him so relentlessly.

When the ship docked in Liverpool, several sailors came up to John. "We were wondering, sir, will you be sailing for Africa again soon?" asked one. "Because if you are, we would be happy to serve under you again."

"Why, I thank you for saying so!" responded John in surprise. "But the fact is, I have some very important business to attend to in Kent. I probably won't be sailing again for quite some time."

When his work in Liverpool was finished, John headed straight for Mary's house in Kent.

"I love you, Mary," John said. "You stood by

me through so many bad times, and you believed in me when everyone else had given up hope. I know that I don't have much to offer you, but if you'll have me, I want you to be my wife."

"I've loved you and prayed for you for eight long years, John," Mary answerd. "God is faithful. He has answered all my prayers for you. I'd be proud to have you for my husband."

And so it was that on February 1, 1750, John Newton and Mary Catlett were married. Their neighbors, friends, and relatives joined them to offer their congratulations and best wishes and to marvel at the change in John. The only one missing was John's father.

"I don't think that there are very many people alive who have known more misery and despair than I have," John told his new bride. "But I don't think that there are many who have ever been happier than I am today, either. My happiness would be complete if my father was here with us."

"You did write and tell him that we would be married today, didn't you?" asked Mary.

"I certainly did," said John. "And he was planning to come back to England in time to be with us. I just can't understand what happened."

Mr. Catlett, who had been strangely silent all day, stepped forward. When he spoke, it was in a strained voice. "John," he said, "I didn't want to do or say anything that would spoil this special day for you. But I guess you do have a right to know the truth. The ship on which your father was to return arrived several days ago."

"You mean my father wasn't on it?" John asked

in surprise. "Do you suppose he missed it? That certainly doesn't sound like him."

"John," said Mr. Catlett quietly, "your father died the day before the ship sailed."

For several moments John stared at him in shocked silence. Then he asked in dismay, "Are you telling me that my father is dead?"

Mr. Catlett nodded.

Filled with overwhelming sadness, John slumped down onto the sofa and buried his face in his hands. Mr. Catlett walked over and put his hand on his son-in-law's shoulder. In a gentle voice he said, "Your father died happy, John. He knew all about the change in you, and he was so pleased. Every one of your letters had reached him, and he saved them all. They were his greatest treasures. All of them had been carefully packed in his suitcase in preparation for his trip home. Your father's last words were, 'Tell my son that I love him very much. I'll see him in heaven.' "

"Don't be so sad, John," Mrs. Catlett added gently. "Your father certainly isn't. He would want you to get on with your new life."

John and Mary Newton spent months setting up their new home. John had not been a part of a real family since he was seven years old, and for him every day was a new adventure. One evening just before bedtime Mary asked, "What's bothering you, John? You've been so quiet and thoughtful all day."

"These months I've spent with you have been the happiest of my entire life," John said slowly. "But it really is time for me to be going back to sea."

For a few minutes Mary said nothing. Though she had known all along that this day would come, she was dreading it. But she was resigned to the fact that John was a sailor, and she knew that being a sailor's wife meant that she should expect to spend most of her time alone.

"When are you leaving?" she asked.

"Next week," John answered. "I knew that you would be disappointed, so I waited until the last possible day to tell you about this."

"Is it another slave ship?" Mary asked.

"Yes," said John. "I know how you feel, Mary, but whether you like it or not, slavery is a fact of life. Africans are going to be brought to civilized countries and sold as slaves. If I don't bring them, someone else will."

Although Mary said nothing, John knew full well that she was not convinced.

"I prayed about it, Mary," he continued. "I asked that God would show me in an unmistakable way if He didn't want me to run a slave ship. Well, He hasn't shown me, so I guess it doesn't matter to Him."

But John was wrong. It did matter to God. And very soon John's prayer was answered in a most unexpected way. Two days before his ship was to sail, John and Mary were sitting together at home enjoying their afternoon tea. All of a sudden John dropped his teacup and fell to the floor. There he lay, unconscious and barely breathing. Mary was terrified. She could do nothing to help him. Though she was afraid to leave him alone, she had no choice. The only doctor was miles away, and Mary had to go get him.

It was over an hour before John finally opened his eyes. Blinking in confusion, he stared up at the doctor and Mary, who were standing over him.

"How do you feel, John?" the doctor asked.

"I—I'm not sure," John said hesitantly. "I'm awfully dizzy, and I have a horrible headache."

"I don't know what's wrong with you," the doctor confessed, "but I can tell you one thing positively. You have no business shipping out to sea in two days!"

John closed his eyes in pain. "I think you're right," he said. "The ship will have to sail without me."

The doctor never was able to explain John's strange illness. Whatever it was, it didn't last long. The very next day he was up and about, and by the end of the week he was his old self again.

It was two weeks after his recovery that John heard the awful news. The ship on which he was supposed to sail had met with high winds and rough, stormy seas. It had immediately filled with water and within minutes had sunk to the bottom of the sea. The man who had taken John's place as captain was dead. So were all of the ship's officers and all but four of the crewmen.

"It's happened again!" John exclaimed. "My life has been miraculously spared by the almighty hand of God!"

"It's like my mother said, John—the Lord is preserving you for some very special reason," Mary said earnestly. "I can hardly wait to see what He has planned for you!"

"I guess you've been right all along about the slave ship," John told his wife. "I prayed that God would give me a sign if He didn't want me in this business, and it certainly does look as if He has answered my prayers."

For a long time John and Mary sat in silence. When John finally spoke, it was slowly and thoughtfully. "I don't think I'll be going back to sea."

"You mean not at all?" Mary asked in surprise.

"Not at all," John answered. "I think God has better plans for my life. And I think it's about time I follow God's plans instead of my own!"

18

What Shall I Do?

"I'm satisfied with the decision to retire from my sailing life," John told Mary, "but I'll have to admit that I'm worried. How am I going to earn a living for us? I've got to get a job soon, but I don't know how to do anything except be a sailor. Why, I don't even know what kind of work I should look for."

"If there's one lesson you should have learned by now, John Newton, it's to trust God to work out these problems," replied Mary with a smile. "We have left this matter in His hands, haven't we? Then we mustn't worry!"

"I know," said John with a sigh. "But it's a whole lot easier to talk about trusting the Lord than it is to actually do it. When my friends in Liverpool offered to get me a job there, I was sure that that was the way God would provide for us."

"Whatever happened about that job?" Mary asked.

"They had already hired someone else," John answered.

"Was it a job you would really have liked?"

"Well, probably not," John answered. "But a job is a job."

"But you don't want just any job, do you?" asked Mary. "Don't you want the special job that God has for you?"

"At this point, any job would be all right with me!" John answered.

"I suppose the reason we complain so much is that we just don't understand the way that the Lord is working with us," Mary said with a sigh. "I know He's doing what's best for us even when we can't make any sense of it. If we could only see the entire picture through His eyes, I know we would rejoice. We wouldn't change a single detail even if we could."

"I suppose that's true," John said. "But I can't help wishing that God would give me a glimpse of that master plan of His. It sure would make my life easier!"

"Oh, John!" Mary laughed. "You can be the most impatient person."

Two days later a messenger knocked at the Newtons' front door. "Letter for Mr. Newton!" he called.

John read the letter carefully, then he ran to find Mary. "I've got a job!" he called. "I've got a job!"

Mary hurried out from the kitchen, wiping her wet hands on her apron. "You got a job?" she asked. "What kind of a job is it?"

"Surveyor," John replied.

"John! Those jobs are hard to get!" Mary exclaimed. "When did you apply for that position? You didn't even tell me about it."

"That's the strange part," John answered. "I didn't apply for it at all. Jobs like this *are* hard to get, but this one—well, it's almost like a gift from heaven."

"I'm sure that's exactly what it is," said Mary with a smile. "Didn't I tell you God would work it out?"

The surveyor's job was a perfect one for John. While it provided him with interesting work, it also allowed him plenty of free time to do the thing that he enjoyed the most—study the Bible.

One day while he was studying, John said, "Listen to these verses I just read in the book of Galatians, Mary—verses twenty-three and twenty-four of chapter of one: 'But they had heard only, That he which persecuted us in times past now preacheth the faith which once he destroyed. And they glorified God in me.' Does that description fit anyone you know?"

"Well, it's talking about the apostle Paul," said Mary.

"Yes, but doesn't it remind you of someone else?" John persisted.

"I know who you're thinking of," said Mary. "You're thinking of yourself, John Newton!"

"I just wish I had a chance to speak publicly for my Lord like Paul did," John said. "I wish I could tell about the difference He has made in my life. What could be a better demonstration of His great mercy and power? My life has been anything but pleasant, and I readily admit that I am the chief of sinners. But still, when I turned to Him for help, God heard me and He saved me.

"When I look back on my wild, sinful life I can very clearly see the way in which the Lord has led me. I'm only just now beginning to understand His great mercy and goodness, which directed me and watched over my every step. Do you remember how I used to think that everything that happened to me was luck—sometimes good and sometimes bad? How wrong I was! Nothing has ever happened to me without a reason. And nothing has ever happened at the wrong time or lasted longer than was necessary. Long before I knew Him, my life was in the hands of my kind, wise, and loving Lord."

"Why, John!" exclaimed Mary. "I do believe your mother was right. You surely do sound like a preacher to me."

"I wish I was a preacher, Mary," John said earnestly. "I really do. It just seems that there are certain people God chooses for the very purpose of proving His boundless grace and the greatness of His mighty power. Those people sin horribly—so much so that one would think that God would remove them from the face of the earth. But He doesn't. In fact, He pursues them. Even though they continue in their wicked rebellion, God refuses to give up on them. Then, when such people have reached the very depths of sin, they turn to God and He saves them. He forgives them for everything, and He makes a new person out of each one of them. And do you know what happens then? They become monuments to the amazing mercy of God.

When others see what God has done for these greatest of sinners, they come to understand that He truly can save anyone."

"Are you thinking of anyone in particular, John?" Mary asked.

"Well, the apostle Paul certainly was one," said John. "And I myself am another."

"Why don't you become a preacher?" asked Mary. "It's obvious that that is what you really want to do. I think you would do an excellent job."

"Not yet," said John. "I don't know enough. There's so much more for me to learn."

"If you wait until you know everything there is to learn, you'll never be ready," said Mary.

John worked hard as a surveyor, and he did his job well. He was also a good and loving husband to Mary. But he always made sure that there was time to devote to studying the Bible.

One evening as John and Mary were eating supper, Mary said, "Some of your friends from church came to the house this morning, John. They seemed very anxious to see you."

"I know," John replied. "They met me this afternoon for tea."

"What did they want?" Mary asked.

"They wanted to talk to me about going into the ministry," said John. "They have mentioned it before, you know, but now they are encouraging me to take some steps toward actually getting started."

"How do you feel about it?" asked Mary.

"Well, you know that there's nothing I would rather do," John said. "And I certainly have given it a lot of thought. But the thing is, God knows that I'm willing to preach. So it seems to me that it would be best to wait and let Him show me the right place and the right time. Maybe I'm still not ready."

After a long pause John added, "But I just can't get around the fact that what I really want to do is tell people about our great God. I want to tell them that if He could save a wicked sinner like John Newton, then He can save anyone."

"I'm sure you will get your chance, John," said Mary. "Just wait. The right time will come, and when it does you will know it."

19

Preacher John

John's desire to preach grew stronger and stronger. Finally he decided that he could wait no longer. On December 16, 1758, John Newton got up the courage to see the Archbishop of York and to ask to be ordained as a preacher for the Church of England. The Archbishop listened politely to John's request, but his answer was a definite no.

"It just isn't the right time, John," Mary said gently when John came home with the disappointing news. "Be patient. Your time will come."

"Will it?" asked John. "I'm not so sure. I'm already thirty-three years old, remember."

John's time did come, but he had to wait another six years. It was in the year 1764 that he was offered the position as pastor of a church—not in Kent, but in the town of Olney. The church was very small when John first arrived, but it grew quickly. Old people and young people alike came from all around to see and to hear this good and gentle man, who had been such a wicked sinner before God saved him. John used his own experiences as examples of God's boundless love and forgiveness.

"When the Lord accepts us into His family, He takes our personalities and our talents into consideration," John told his congregation. "He allows different situations and problems to occur in our lives and He appoints us to different jobs and responsibilities.

"Everyone has some trials and tribulations during his lifetime, some more and some less. While God allows some of us to sail through life quite smoothly and easily, others are tossed roughly about the seas of life, sometimes suffering so greatly that we almost give up hope. What is important is that we never lose sight of the fact that God is doing what is best for each one of His children. He won't allow a single one of them to perish in life's storms.

"And you must remember this—never think that you can share someone else's experience or that anyone can share yours. I'm sure you will all agree that my own case is extremely unusual. Very few have come to the Lord after sinking as low as I did. When I consider God's boundless mercy to me, I can only bow before Him in humble gratitude."

Another time John told his people, "We are God's children, and He deals with us in the same way that we deal with our own children. First He speaks to us. If we won't listen, He gives us a gentle stroke. Then, if we still won't listen, He gives us a hard blow. That's exactly what He had to do to me."

John Newton was as happy with his life as a preacher as his congregation was happy with him.

He worked hard, and he studied hard. He loved God, and he loved his people.

In those days most people thought of church merely as a place to worship God, to listen to a sermon, and to pray together for an hour or so on Sunday morning. The church had no place in their lives during the rest of the week. But John Newton thought that was wrong. He wanted more than that for his people. He wanted the church to be a place where they could truly come to know the Lord, where they could develop a closer personal relationship with Him. So John Newton did many things that most pastors of those days had never tried.

There had never been anything at church especially for children, so John started a Sunday school for them. And since he believed so strongly in the power of prayer, John held four special prayer meetings every week. Two of them met on Sunday—one at six in the morning and the other at eight in the evening; and two met on Tuesdays—one at five in the morning and the other at eight in the evening.

"Our people surely do love to sing," John commented to his wife one day. "It's too bad that there are so few hymns and Christian songs for us to use in our prayer meetings."

"Why don't you write some?" Mary suggested. "You have a real way with words. I think that you could be a very good hymnwriter."

"Hm," said John thoughtfully. "Well, now, it just might be fun to try at that. In fact, I think I'll work on one for this Tuesday night."

John's new hymn was so well received that he decided to write a new one every week. Some of them he wrote himself, and some were written by William Cowper, a poet who was a member of his congregation. During his fifteen years at Olney, John Newton wrote over three hundred hymns for his church to sing. And with Mr. Cowper he published a hymnbook so that other churches could also use the hymns.

After fifteen years under John Newton's leadership, the church at Olney had grown quite large. Then one day in the summer of 1779, a good friend of John's—a very important man from London—came to see him. The man's name was Mr. Thornton.

"John," he said, "we have a church in London that badly needs a great preacher like you. Would you be willing to move up there and take that church?"

For a long time John and Mary thought about the offer. Together they discussed the move and what it would mean.

"I love our church here in Olney," John said to Mary. "Our years here have been such happy ones, and the Lord certainly has blessed our work. If we were to move away I know that we would miss our friends terribly. Still, I can't help but think how good it would be to get back to London again."

"It just may be that you have finished the work that God had for you here," said Mary. "If you decide that it would be best to move, then I won't object."

After a great deal of prayer, John wrote to London with this answer: "I appreciate your invitation to come to London to be the pastor of Saint Mary Woolnoth Church. It is with pleasure that I am accepting your offer."

It was hard for John and Mary Newton to say good-by to their many friends, but the decision had been made, and they felt certain that it was what the Lord wanted them to do. Saint Mary Woolnoth Church, located in the very heart of the great city of London, was a big change from the country church in the small town of Olney. On December 9, 1779, John preached his first sermon there.

"The people here are much wealthier and more fashionable than the people at Olney," John once said. "But there are two things that are true of all people no matter who they are. One is that all are sinners, and the other is that the Word of God is equally true for everyone, everywhere. Some of you asked me if I will preach differently here than I did at Olney. The answer is absolutely not! Why should I? God's message is still the same."

John's new position was an important one, a fact that constantly amazed him. "It just doesn't seem possible," he said shaking his head in wonder. "Imagine! Me, the most ignorant, the most wicked, the most miserable of slaves! How could it be that I was rescued from all of that and then was allowed to minister at this magnificent church in the greatest city in the whole world? It truly doesn't seem possible. Who could doubt that I am a living testimony to the amazing grace of our great God?"

Though the neighborhood was a wealthy one, John made sure that Saint Mary's Church was open to all people, no matter who they were. Many rich and important people attended the church, but there were also the poor, the sick, and the lonely. These people found in Pastor John Newton the comfort and the sympathy that they could find nowhere else. He was like a father leading, guiding, and teaching his children. He also made a special effort to encourage younger ministers and those who were interested in becoming ministers.

John and Mary Newton never moved again. John served as the pastor at Saint Mary Woolnoth Church for the rest of his life, and many, many people came to know Jesus Christ as their personal Savior because of John's powerful preaching and his loving and faithful ministry.

20

Amazing Grace

Mary Newton died in December of 1790. Even in his deep grief, however, John continued to preach. He didn't miss a single Sunday.

But John Newton was growing old. His hearing and his eyesight were both beginning to fail, and he could no longer walk without a cane. Finally, by the time he was eighty years old, his sight had become so weak that he could no longer read his sermon notes to the congregation.

"Perhaps it's time for you to retire," some of his friends gently suggested. "You have served God well for many years now, and you deserve a rest. Why not quit while you can still have a little time to spend on yourself?"

"What?" shouted John. "Should this old slave ship captain who hated God for so long stop preaching while he can still speak? Never! Never, never, never!"

The suggestion made John so angry that no one ever dared to say such a thing again. And John did continue to preach, but now a helper sat next to him on the church platform to read his notes to him.

One Sunday morning in December, when he was eighty-two years old, John Newton said to his congregation, "God is infinitely wise and infinitely good. In my own life I have found that it is not possible for me to change any detail of God's plan. Even if I could change it, I would only end up spoiling it. Such a foolish creature as I am, so blind to the consequences of my own wishes, how could it be possible for me to choose for myself? What a great privilege, what an indescribable mercy, that the Lord God stooped down and chose me!

"My dear friends, my memory is now almost gone. But there are two things that I can still remember perfectly well. I can remember what a great sinner I was, and I can remember what a great Savior Christ Jesus is!"

That was the last sermon ever preached by John Newton. Four days before Christmas, in the year 1807, his condition grew so serious that the doctor sent for John's closest friends to come and be with him.

"It's very unlikely that he will live through the night," the doctor told them. "I called all of you because John has been asking to see you all one more time."

John Newton looked at his dear friends who were gathered around his bed. When he saw the tears in their eyes and the sadness on their faces he said, "Why should you all be so sad? Don't you realize that when I shut my eyes on this world for the last time I will open them to a far better one? What a wonderful thing it is to live under the shadow of the protective wings of the Almighty God."

"Yes, God is gracious," whispered one of the men beside him.

"If He weren't," replied John, "how could I dare to stand before Him?"

Those were John Newton's last words. He died that night with a smile on his lips. He had been waiting so long to see his Savior face to face.

One of John Newton's best loved hymns tells us how he felt about a Savior so great the He could save even a cruel, wicked slave ship captain. John wrote the words, and today we sing them to the tune of an old American slave song. This hymn is called "Amazing Grace."

Amazing Grace! How sweet the sound
  That saved a wretch like me!
I once was lost, but now am found,
  Was blind, but now I see.

'Twas grace that taught my heart to fear,
  And grace my fears relieved.
How precious did that grace appear
  The hour I first believed!

Through many dangers, toils and snares,
  I have already come;
'Tis grace that brought me safe thus far,
  And grace will lead me home.

When we've been there ten thousand years,
  Bright shining as the sun,
We've no less days to sing God's praise
  Than when we'd first begun.

Moody Press, a ministry of the Moody Bible Institute, is designed for education, evangelization, and edification. If we may assist you in knowing more about Christ and the Christian life, please write us without obligation: Moody Press, c/o MLM, Chicago, Illinois 60610.